Blue-bird sings the Blues

Also by Noël Sweeney

An Animals' Charter

Doris and the Grumpy Judge

English Hungers

In Defence of Bees

A Practical Approach to Animal Welfare Law

Animals-in-Law

Dogs of Law

Bees-at-Law

Blue-bird sings the Blues

Noël Sweeney

This edition was first published in Great Britain in 2021
by Alibi an imprint of Veritas Chambers
Unit 4 + 1 BP Bristol

A catalogue record for this book is available from the British Library.

ISBN 978-1-872724-30-0

Dedication

To Joan and Wendy and Maureen and Polly and Pop and Cecil and their forever faithful friends who further than most saw the rare ghost of fleeting justice. Long may they hold a candle that burns to illuminate our bleakest hour and tower. There is no change. They saw and see the true face within each space. All they needed is their vision to realise the wisest eyes may be closed yet wide. That remains the same with the passing of time and each toll that chimes with the changing tide. Still they listen intently to the rare and raw singing of the whale and the wild whistling wind.

Acknowledgements

The wordsmiths that float across any furrowed brow are too many to mention. Those that remain are far fewer. Ones that come to mind are Blake whose pure voice resonates on so many portentous levels. Clare is also there because he captured the feeling of being one who saw the badger as an image and reflection of his captive self. The call to arms of Oliver drifts off the page with a quiet rage long after her ideas have cast a spell while filtering into life. Together they provide a map and a sign of the distance we have to cover to try to discover a purpose worth pursuing. May their counterpart strike some sparks for the solid soul and sound of Samuel Sharpe so where justice is denied she never commits the crime of cute cowardice or the original sin by silence. May they have the strength to see the sight and follow the blinding light of Martha White. On the darkest night Martha hid her fear so it disappeared into the shadow where it belonged. All she needed was another heart to hear. They prove the reason to protest and survive while staying alive. The 2021 football team took a prescient step towards BLM which should lead to the next step on our rugged road towards ALM.

Contents

The Serial Culler

Red River Running

Cull-me-to-You

How to be a Rodeo Hero

Words will never hurt Me

A Claim to a Name

The Pangolin's Saviour

The Price of a Pangolin

A Zoonotic Reservoir

Food for Thought

Let's all go to the Zoo

Job's Cat

The Fish that failed to Scream

The Palace of Plunder Land

A Whale of a Time

Silence of Science

The Lawyer loved lager and Lime

A Trophy for Vanity

Sticks in your Stomach

A Colston con meets a sapient Swan

Law and life and logic and Love

One and two and Zero

The law of Italian Love

Please pass the Sandwich

Fit as a butcher's Dog

A Dog is just for the Pandemic

Shylock's Blood

The Missionary and the Cannibal

From BLM to ALM Stem-by-Stem

Marooned rats leave the Ship

A Shark in shallow Waters

Cycle of Life

Voyage of *The Zong*

Tulsa Massacre Anniversary 1921-2021

White is right about being Black

Blank Heart of a Hunter

Blue-bird sings the Blues

Preface

God is so wise that when she created birds she gave them complete freedom from the invisible chains of the sky. We are so wise that we prove our natural love of birds by confining them in cramped cages. Her spirit sailed through the swirling sea making it so wide that fish would be forever free. We value fish by catching them in the net of crime and time to place them in our holy prison of piracy and endless fiddle-de-dee.

Yet the lesson of dignity and respect due to the reason animals inhabit the world is all around us. They were here long before us and will remain when our epitaphs are hidden by wind-blown unkempt sprawling weeds.

One who knew that unassailable truth is a French woman who, when she heard the word, sided with and chided her husband to rescue an injured bird. Stephane Mahe witnessed how Xavier Bouget was accompanied by Blanchon, a white female pigeon, as he tended to his daily duties including nibbling on a hobnob, watering his garden and tinkering in his workshop. She was even by his side when he cycled in the countryside. Blanchon is always there. She was befriended by Bouget when she was a frightened chick. Now she has become his constant companion. She perches parrot-style on his shoulder as well as walking with him. They met when Bouget saw her trying to escape from a cat. He went home and told his wife what he saw. She chided him on why he had not rescued the bird. So he went back, did so and took Blanchon home in his pocket. Everyone now asks him how he trained the bird to be so tame. He explains 'there is no trick just mutual respect'. He claims anyone can do the same if 'they respect the animal for what it is, that is a living creature that shares the Earth with us.'

Bouget said, 'You just need to be patient, to understand how they live and adapt to their life, because they will adapt to yours.' We have a lot to learn from him as he willingly shared the wisdom of his grand age, having lived for eight decades.

Whether it is true or merely covered by the dust of rumour is not the crucial issue when it was claimed that Obama said of another politician that 'I didn't think we'd have a racist sexist pig in Office.' Regardless of any claim to defame another political pawn in a faker's game, the crucial issue is a pig faces a stun gun let alone a knife that can and does take his life. Nor does it sit easily with prejudice to black people and women when at a stroke the aim and approach targets the wrong victim of prejudice.

Any which way anyone sings that same song, they are certainly wrong to woefully try gaining a dig by decrying a pig. Perhaps we could learn from an arrogant American politician who railed against a bunch of arsonists whom he condemned as acting like 'animals'.

Whatever else might be validly critically aimed at animals, it is misconceived to brand them as criminals. Equally the mouthy politician, as if there was another kind, might learn from the fact that animals merely wish to live in their natural surroundings and not be troubled by myopic humans who judge others by themselves.

Baldwin's declaration that 'I am not your Negro' applies to the blackboard jungle for humans. Equally the claim applies in the universal jungle for animals.

Birds of all descriptions have always been abused by us. The twisted creeps who trap birds with a sticky lime to the use them as decoys to trap other bigger birds show the callous core of our vulture society dressed up and surpassed in a mismatched attempt to pass it off as culture. It is no different than the Birdman of Alcatraz who was acclaimed for his rehabilitative venture. Yet while he was incarcerated because he had committed a crime, what crime had the birds he used in his 'research' committed except for their nature's fortune in being born?

It resonates with the vicars gathering at Christmas where the various birds disappear as swiftly as if they had voluntarily flown down the diners' throats. Much like the rattling coins in their collection plate, the birds are devoured as if they were a gift from God.

Feminism is a false philosophy because many if not most do not give a second thought to the plight of animals and their lack of legal rights. Where animals are concerned women who are professed feminists have not learned the base of and reason for feminism.

Sexism is base because it discriminates against humans purely as a matter of biology. Husbands once had the same feeling endorsed by law in regard to the prized possession of their wives. It was sexism meets speciesism. For the same reason feminism remains as false and true as an honest politician.

It is magnified in sharp focus by the self-proclaimed feminist Caitlin Moran who boasted in 2015 about her feelings towards her 'rescued' cat, Betty: 'I am a cat hater. I hate my cat...God, I hate that cat.' She devoted her complete column to the same theme. Later in 2019 she referred to how she had been told by her father to kill a fish.

As a child she accompanied him on a fishing trip until the day 'a gudgeon swallowed the hook too enthusiastically making it impossible to get out'. He told her to kill the fish. He 'barked' at her: 'Do it! It's in *agony*. *Finish it off*!' She tried to 'stove its head in' with a rubber torch. Following that childhood 'traumatic experience' she quit fishing. Until that is in 2019 when as a mature adult she was 'eager to show off my skills' yet again.

The view of Alice Walker says all that a genuine feminist needs to know to be true to their self: 'The animals of the world exist for their own reasons. They were not made for humans any more than black people were made for whites or women for men.'

Helen Jones shared that wisdom. She quit a body that was concerned with 'welfare' and decided to fight for animal 'rights'. From quitting a body she believed was impotent she set up the most vital organization for animal rights in the world.

Women should not have power over men, but over themselves. Baldwin saw the connection between racism and sexism and speciesism. In that context it is peculiar that a previous prime minister, Theresa May, was in favour of changing the law to revive hunting foxes to death for fun.

The same policy has been adopted by a present politician, Liz Truss. With an irony even an opponent could not generate she is now the 'minister for women and equalities'. Proof if it were needed that the only person to trust less than a politician is two of them. Meanwhile their ephemeral promises prove that animals are legal canaries in our social mines.

The same clarion call could be made by every silent animal, entities in their own right, who need to live and die on their terms. That is why her timeless tune is proof the blue-bird was born to sing. Yet all it takes is a single shot from the one with a sawn-off soul who blasts her from the blood-spilled skies. It is not hard to figure that regardless of who is the one that holds the gun, we use our shared vision and vigour to pull the trigger.

Blue-bird Poems and Miscellany

Furnace in June

Fear-filled faces pressed hard
Against the misty windows
Their screams split the sky
From midnight 'til noon
While the wild wind fanned flames
That trapped the unnamed who
Fried alive inside
The Furnace in June

The lady with dementia
Couldn't open the door
While her parrot roared 'fire!'
That cracked a mournful tune
No place to escape
As the flamed curtains draped they
Fried alive inside
The Furnace in June

The family huddled tight
Through their last long night
As blades of the blaze
Hit harder than a whale's harpoon
Choked back by black smoke
Goldfish drowned in a sea of fire they
Fried alive inside
The Furnace in June

The man in the wheelchair
With his mog on his lap
And his dog at his feet
Soon found none were immune
Their fur torched by flames
While he cried out their names they
Fried alive inside
The Furnace in June

Many people's tears
Washed blue-birds in their cage
Their wet feathers ashes and
Foam flowers formed a dune
Amidst the cindered embers
Inferno graves for those who
Fried alive inside
The Furnace in June

Politicians all talked
Clown councillors walked
Heard screaming rabbits on fire
Failing to read the runes
Closed eyes and closed minds
While people and pets died all
Fried alive inside
The Furnace in June

Mama, will they spurn us
Will this cauldron burn us?
Children cried in the furnace
Gerbils framed by flamed festoons
Mama, does anyone care?
When the answer was bare they
Fried alive inside
The Furnace in June

All the pale poseurs
Joined political pygmies
Spit their litany of lies
A parade of poltroons
If rough justice rings true
They will be the ones who are
Fried alive inside
The Furnace in June

No one counts those who died
Human and animal apartheid
Forgotten by phoneys as
Profits was their only boon
Numbers on the pyre
As bodies piled higher they
Fried alive inside
The Furnace in June

Pets and people in cold graves
When flames doused their cries
Burning arrows head to toe
Beneath a pale shadowed moon
Together they shivered
In the fierce fiery river they
Fried alive inside
The Furnace in June

Politicians played to forget
The people and their pets
Whose fixed fate was forged
By the blind buffoons
All bluster and bluff
Too many was not enough then
Fried alive inside
The Furnace in June

The mountain of lies
While bodies multiplied
Adding to the cladding
Of the fiery typhoon
More people and pets
Cracked a death choir then
Fried alive inside
A Furnace next June

Seventy two lost souls
Fought fate's fading spark
Noah's Ark in the dark
Set adrift and marooned
The justice-seat is sutured
Your past is their future to be
Fried alive inside
A Furnace next June

A Catechism Creed

John Smith was just a child
When his father taught him
How to shoot deer in the wild
Killing both of them with vim

When he shot a bird of paradise
As she fell he felt pure guilt
A flood of tears filled his eyes
His conscience bit him to the hilt

John Smith went into the box
To make his first confession
Said his conscience still rocks
The priest then ruined the session

He said concern for a bird
You have no reason for guilt
Caring for a pox is so absurd
When birds are only flying silt

John Smith knew that his religion
Had no place in his wounded heart
Without care for a wounded pigeon
His start backed the horse not the cart

The priest in that first confession
Taught him a lasting life lesson
One that he would never forget
He learned the cost of compassion

When no one counts in any amount
Life has its own price for each debt
Yet it remains one that has to be repaid
Yes it remains a debt that must be met

All animals are our heaven's gift
We do not have to steal or lift
We do not have to sort or sift
Seeing his eyes skyward shift
The child saw the priest's drift

Selling his story as a narcotic for many
Given free as the people's natural dope
The priest paraded a prayer for a penny
Granted by each pope as new old rope

Sold with the chalice from a gilded palace
Selling a blessed sight of food as their hope
Just another well-timed evangelistic trope
As vital as a vision in a broken periscope

Our Holocaust Sacrifice

The inside of a circle
That passes through a hole
Emits the same emptiness
That passes through each soul
Denying without buying a truth
Becomes the primary reason
Of our each nature's season
Is met by our nature's treason
Of those whose purpose is to serve
Killing them to satisfy a craving
As for us no life of theirs
Can ever be worth saving
Each one born for our use
Though we know it is no excuse
While we tightly tie the loose noose
To avoid being discovered or defrocked
Or excommunicated for having rocked
A foundation stone of our history holocaust
Before its current claim had an unpaid cost
Where millions of animals were slaughtered
Mere merchandise in our religious sacrifice
We can forget the timely commercial gloss
Knowing silence is our only riposte
For the 8 million horses purposely lost
Becoming a pile of our war's compost

Abandoned and shot and starved in permafrost
Without feeling for our gift-free Pentecost
Who we then casually tossed
Into the bullet-spun cauldron
Like the origin of killing on our altar
With no reason for us to halt or falter
In using a 'whole burnt' animal sacrifice
Their death's no less than their life's price
A religious practice we have yet to exhaust
As we continue killing the unwilling
It is a doddle using them as cannon fodder
In our World War Animal holocaust

Stag-spanner Ambush at Wounded Knee

The Apache Bison surveyed the scene
Champing at the bit and mustard-keen
Seeing the desolation devil cavalry
Sharpening swords and war cry words
Along with pistols and random riflery
Each rival ready for some savagery

The Bison were on the horizon
Looking down on the long drop
Ready to deliver their poison
Seeing soldiers circled in sizzling billets
Waiting to pump their repeater bullets
The Bison knew were meant for them
The Bison knew were to be their requiem

The Stag-spanners grouped on the hill
Awaiting with the Geronimo scouts
Searching for the poised soldiers
Perched ready to take them all out
Watching for the gathering Bison
Rising on the hazy mirage horizon
They signalled to the Comanche Deer
Concealed behind the camouflage trees
Deep within the highest brambles
Keeping their hungry spirit alive
Among the swarming angry hive
Of wild-eyed Cheyenne Bees

Chief Cochise Stag lifted her foot
Towards the hidden Navajo Foxes
Hiding their brush in the bush
Preparing for their final push
While the signal passed down the line
From Cherokee Boar to Boar
Ready for the rush when they roared
A marauding band of Animals-of-War

Starting with a grunting chunter
The sound echoed around the ground
Instilling fear within the soldier hunters
Intending to wreak their wanton will
Fired dragons surrounding the wagons

As they charged towards the punters
Wild Dove saw the ones who hunted her
Full of fright they dropped their smoking guns
Seeing the marauding mass Apache hunters
They had an instant case of the severe runs

The smell of fear overcame them all
As hooves and legs and cloudy galloping paws
Thundered down on them as death's call
A mirror-image of Draconian Stag-spanner laws

Each and every hungry human hunter
Feeling they had nowhere left to hide
Their scared eyes timed to meet their demise
The pounding hounds ripped out their insides
Left them to rot in their skins on the lonesome field
Where once they stood proud now could only yield
So where they once stood they now died
Each and every hunter lay in their blood
Each and every Native Animal felt the flood
Flowing through their scorched veins
Seeing that justice was truth in action
Proclaimed in the hunters remains
In that moment the Native Animals knew
All they had done was exercise their will
To understand what for hunters was a thrill
To examine why their lives
Counted for little or nothing
In the soldier blues' eyes
Before their brutal death arrives

It was plain on the Plains for all to see
The glory of their epitaph on Wounded Knee
They understood what the hunters meant
By the unspoken thrill of the unfolding event
The longed-for scene that nothing could prevent
Stag-spanners scruples stayed crooked and bent

The Stag-spanners felt no pity
Killing for a cold revenge
As minds and hearts were singed
Stag-spanners as the Angels of Avenge
Picking up the guns scattered around
The debris on the blood-filled ground
Seeing the wounded hunters
Spread-eagled in a pungent blur
Amid a blood-pooled violent sea
Finished each one off with a bullet
As a final act of reverse mercy
Just to put them out of their misery

They said on the tombstone:
The undiluted truth plain to see
Of their human epitaph on Wounded Knee
Animals behaved worse than animals
Animals behaved just like animals
Yet they forgot what was seminal
The animals behaved like criminals
With strength that seemed superhuman
From start to finish they were inhuman
A lesson they learned from the humans

The cavalry lying head to head
Eyes closed forever in fear
As each warriors' kick struck
The vanquished ran out of luck
Just like every captured criminal
Just like every captured animal
Birth as a mark of guilt in the dark
No light in their fight for life's spark
There was one point that mattered
The criminal had committed a crime
Some lives were constantly battered
Some lives were simply shattered
Some received their dues to save time
Yet the Stag-spanners were shorn
Of any defence to their crime
A cardinal one of simply being born

The Sioux Badgers were up all night
They were still hankering for a fight
None of them were tired
All of them were wired
They could take on any cavalry dog
Easier than rolling off a floating log
So every baiter was just another hater
That deserved to be caught and served
Between the Badger's vice-like jaws
Who were sure they had a cause

For they thought and often fought
For their stranded lives
Until the terrier man arrives
Then they smashed each face
And laughed as is commonplace
Well now they had a lesson
Direct from nature's delicatessen
This time we are not messing
This is your final tender blessing
Like us before this is your last door
So as your destiny awaits be ready to die
It is too late for your bleeding pleading cry

The Seminole Beavers were at the bank
Ready to make the hunters' lives blank
Preparing to make them walk the plank
Seeing the Beavers made their hearts tank
Each was holding a sharp cleaver
Each red-hot with a red-coat fever
One-by-one the hunters simply fell
One-by-one into the drink and dell
Beavers clamped their feet on their teeth
Giving the hunters someone new to meet
The waters opened in a feral flood
Floating on top was their oily blood
Turning turtle as with the Beavers before
The hunters were knocking on hell's door
Their every last gurgle and bubble
As they bought the fruit of trouble
They had started in the avenging wend
Now they were there at their very end

Iroquois Hares hid in the hedge
Waiting just waiting on the edge
For the signal to be given to break out
For they were enraged waiting to clout
Every type and any kind of courser
Would soon be forced by him and her
Black Eagle gathered in a Crow battalion
Waiting as a bunch of palomino stallions
Hundreds of Hares as an animal army
Ready to course the cruel coursers
Ready to hang on their jutting jugulars
Poised to chase the long-time burglars
Then just when they least expected
They grabbed them around their prospect
With teeth sharper than they suspected
Nipped their member below the plimsoll line
As if it was a shrivelled cud for them to dine
Then when their victims' screams
Filled their daytime nightmare dreams
The army of Hares were unleashed
The hunters screeched and screeched
Yet the Hares were so taken with the gaff
Played it rough and tough
Figuring it was about enough
To make a Cherokee cat laugh

Blackfoot Squirrels made their play
Cyril the squirrel was made that day
It was a pure pleasure as he was grey

So unlike the much favoured red
The cavalry saw him as good as dead
But the scene was great
For the shock that lay in wait
As the reds and greys were best mates
They met on the battlefield wheels
Rolling as they took their last squeals
Then red Beryl joined the Squirrels
Even grey Daryl joined the Squirrels
They were neither feared
Nor worried by being scared
As the bounced around the fences
Ready to deliver the sentence
The air was heavy and intense
Stag-spanners striking out in self-defence

The Stag-spanners circled the wagons
While crouching hunters hid behind
A blind row of real-life snap-dragons
Praying the Angels would change their mind
As Apaches defending their land
In a way the hunters had not planned
With a force borne of revenge
Too late for them to scavenge
For the Trail of Tears centuries of abuse
Now the tables turned and fortune burned
Now they would not listen to any excuse
As they charged and killed the hunters
Seeing just a bunch of losing punters
Their victims' lives flashed by
In the wink of a changing sky

When the Apache Native Animals learned
Something that was of lasting concern
Why did hunters see their blood spilled
Was a befitting prize which just filled
Their hearts with a raw pleasure
To boast about their trophy treasure
Now all at once the Stag-spanners were shown
That which they never could have known
By stealing the hunters crooked will
Led to the war ambush's outstanding bill

The Apache Bison surveyed the scene
Awash with the spreading scarlet stream
Of spent bullets and swirling blood
Floating in a silver sea of misery
Mixing their last memories in the mud
So clear even the blind could see

The Apaches could answer the question
That had long foxed them all
Way past the auto-suggestion
That had led to the devil cavalry's fall
They discovered when forced to swallow
One more variety of life's bitter pill
It was not hard to follow
Though the truth was hollow

As the human blood
Flowed on and on in the mud
As hard as it was for them to say
As the bodies stayed where they lay
With no one left alive to dispute
The feeling of a prophet and a prostitute
The same in the game of each examined life
Between the afterlife and the wildlife
Exactly as the devil cavalry they slaughtered
From a fixed mind to a blocked aorta
Little White Dove became the hangman's daughter
From Blackfoot to Cheyenne each woman and man
Every tribe from Choctaw to Cree had a secret plan
That was now out in the open as they met Jim Crow
From Waco to Winnebago from Comanche to Crow
As the wild animal tribes bathed and basked
Seeking the answer they had all long asked
Their unvarnished wish and unleashed will
That sprung straight out of history's wisdom
Chief Legal Beagle Hawkwind of the Choctaw
Who had practised law and studied the legend
Of Plutarch and Pythagoras via a vestal Virgil
Discovered a truth that was a frozen codicil
They loved the sheer chilled thrill of the kill

They held a powwow to try and discover
Why the cavalry were intent on destruction
What they found in their pipes of peace
Made them wonder if they would ever cease
As demolition and death and spoils of war
Gave them more satisfaction than construction

When Little White Dove held the gun
Something lit within her
Making her totally undone
Before her closed eyes she realised
Balanced against the flame and function
Much as the cowboys wanted to destroy
She knew her tribe was snared too
By the sour-sweet seduction of destruction

A Black Cat Photograph

They do not photograph well at all
When you want to boast
A black cat is just toast
It blends in with the background
So it just becomes a dark rebound
And affects your profile on the social
So you seem to be a bit parochial
And who wants any chit-chat
From a troll for choosing a black cat
Better to go for one who is an aristocrat

You want a thing that looks good
In the photograph as it should
So give the sad black cat a miss
Turn away and never turn back
Because no creature ever looks good
In a photo or a shoot if it is black

You better turn off and turn your back
It is better with one that is white
You can even see them at night
And no one gets bad luck or a fright

While a cat you have to feed each day
It is not worth it what you have to pay
Because they become a messy mound
Whether at the back or in the foreground
On several levels you are much better off
Walking on and leaving the litter behind
Tomorrow you could get a ginger one with a bell
Or maybe a tabby or even a striped tortoiseshell
It is so much easier to clothe them for fun
Yes you can dress them up for a belly-laugh
The bonus is they make a great photograph

It is a bit like an ageing seaside beauty queen
No one wants to choose an acne-ridden teen

Though we do not kill the contestants
We could choose that course for cats
Not unlike most animal sanctuaries do
When we say 'not today'
To any cat that is black
Then walk away and never look back
The sanctuary and cat can take the fall
Remember it is only an animal after all

If people were selected
So those too ugly to live
Were instantly rejected
Who among the rabble
Would ever be elected
Who would a hungry hobo
Or a blind beggar choose
Among our batch of politicos
If she wanted desperate alms
To cross her upturned palm
Might she then perhaps even prefer
A jet black cat in a cellar at midnight
Straight as a razor with her honest purr

If everyone rejects the black cat
In no time the sanctuary will fall
Then we will have a better choice
When the black cats all go to the wall
Their lives are mapped out in our graph
We need a cat for a laugh in a photograph

Even a black cat is okay in its own way
Much as a stuffed panda or teddy bear
But when it gets old and scraggy
With mangy fur and a body that is baggy
Much as with some old coffin-dodger
Whose use is passed as he has had his day
Passed their sell-by date as a lifetime-lodger

You can hand him back because he is black
He could find bliss in a hospice
As any cat that has had their day
Or if that is too much trouble
Add it to the rubble and slowly walk away

Until the cows do not come Home

Some people see a cow as sacred
See something within their form
Making them somehow special
Turning them into a kind of deiform

Yet he saw each cow as ugly
Saw something within their form
That made each one uglier than him
Using it as a disguise to misinform

He called the politician 'a fat cow'
Saw something in their rotund form
Making them as useful and useless
As a politician with a brainstorm

The rapist called his victim a cow
Learning to use their huge form
As abuse from a woman to an animal
His guilt as a transferred platform

Their sleazy words of hate as split silk
Shows their boast has a value of their ilk
They do not know you cannot kill the cow
Then quench a thirst by drinking their milk

Calling out a Cow

Given she is a politician
Why object to repetition
Why object to being called fat
When most of us are just that
Or was it the fact it has a ring
Through her nose
Rather than holding a rose
So that was the thing

The drunken politician lingers too long
Using self-engendered power too much
Places the sober victim in his clutch
Balancing by a hand on her crutch
When she resists he calls her a cow
His sweaty palms and wrinkled brow
Spitting lies through an alcoholic mist
To deliver his halitosis Iscariot kiss

With his nicotine-stained breath
He brands every woman a cow
When she tries to resist his sweat
An ego-tipsy lawyer says 'she's a sow'
Matches his mouth with paltry power
Calling every pupil a diesel dyke cow
Even his huggery is close to buggery
While his sugary words smell sour

Why object to being called fat
When most of us are just that
Did the ring remind her of an auction
Seeing herself as someone's luncheon

Each of them sees the cowed cow
As something they can transform
Into their own rust-worn image
With a closet mental chloroform

The Serial Culler

The empty promise full of bull
Formed from a matching mind
Of false ideals as truth gone blind
Lost in a way they will never find
It counts for little as another lull
All it adds up to is another cull

The numbers are too many
So we have to find a way
To get rid of the past and the pest
That threatens to eat our hay
And eat into our profits and sales
Run them off our land with rails
A speeding shot will silence their wails

Who can object when the victim
Cannot avoid what will hit him
While our only motive is money
That jangles as we talk and walk
Send them to their deaths in cages
As our pellets of poison rages
Through their open veins
In the end all that remains
Will be a mounting mountain heap
Of the red and the dead six feet deep

With souls emptier than a broken drum
Our pockets jingle and our profits hum
As another bound silent victim
Whose lifeline grows forever dim
Caught in the cross-hair cull
As she lines up to take her turn
The target for the marksman's yearn
Spins out of control as the deed is done
To deny her another day in the sun
When as killer and culler
Our lives are much fuller
When we proudly become one

Red River Running

The government claim
They will quit culling
After a few more years
So voters and supporters
And mad Stag-spanners
Will have no reason for tears
Quelling their confused fears
No one will need
To have a troubled thought
Float across a mixed-up head
The government will fidget
As they run out of targets
Before they run out of lead
Though a new one will be bred
From all the rest
That we can deem a pest
So we will need more caskets
For all the extra culprits
We name in our next junket
However we fudge it
To add to the budget
As all the mines are closed
Honey bees and the land
We will kill by an overdose

All our toxic rivers
Will be deadly still
Yet shallow and running red
As the last gasping badger
No longer on political probation
And no need for her perturbation
For the river is her grave
Running and spreading red
As each marked bullet sped
So her life is shed
Spread on a river bed
Just as we always willed
Stilled with a blood rivulet
A bullet lodged in her head
She lies filled with our lead

Cull-me-to-You

The petals of the purple pansy
Used with a straight intention
Sends a scent with that intent
So nature needs no invention

Yes the flower smells sweetly
Except when what is false
Soon shifts to become true
Then the ones who choose
Which ones will be the ones to lose
Smell stronger than a Cull-me-to-You

Only a lonely victim whose lifeline fades
From being dim to a new place in Shittim
As the sure hot shot is certain to hit him
All caught in the marksman's cross-hair cull
Where more and more animals and flowers
Add up to the mathematics of our finest hour
It is high Noon as all we can possibly devour
Dying by our hands proves we are successful
Rotting bodies show no reason to be rueful

Each weak one we destroy is proof of what is true
Killing without kindness is our perfect Cull-me-to-You

How to be a Rodeo Hero

How brave he is when he ropes a calf
Uses strength to bring her to the ground
Then stretches her neck nearly in half
Her breathing fear is the loneliest sound

How brave he is when he ropes a steer
When the hungry crowd roars and hollers
Using his force to overcome her fear
Then he makes a few more grubby dollars

How brave he is when he brings her down
Looking into her bulging pleading eyes
As she struggles and stays silently bound
He catches a glimpse of truth where she lies

The rodeo man with his big hat and no cattle
The rodeo man with a head full of empty rattle
The rodeo man who is always ready for battle
Sees his glass face in the dust
Recognises his mirrored lust
Knows too well she was his chattel
When used his twisting ropy prattle
To redeem his circle of tittle-tattle
He leaves her in a pool

For her fluids have no stopcock
Her grazed eyes glazed in shock
The rodeo rider hones his honesty
Placing his conscience in hock
Turns and twists with practised schlock
The rodeo man shows might is right
Using a creature strapped and capped
With no thought to her peril or plight
When the fun ends she is swiftly zapped

The faded blue jeans of eternal youth
Dangling cigarette hides an ominous truth
No saddle needed by the cowboy sooth
Sealing a dream for the forever uncouth

He stands as strong as a wind-blown dandelion
He brands her with a white-hot scalding slave iron
Holding her life in his hands on the ground
His boot heels held fast in the dust she lies on
His strength on her neck steals her breath
His buckle and knuckle invites her death

Later alone he looks at the night sky
He knows how he feels can never fly
Too many questions beg for an answer
He has run out of every reason to lie
Holding truth's secret as his heart's secret
Hidden except during his soul's dark night
He seeks to show how his might is right
He ought to know only right makes might

Words will never hurt Me

She called her fast friend a pig
Because it was so sexist
Demeaned her with a chosen word
Showing how bias is kissed
Then dismissed her as a bitch
Because it was so sexist
Knowing that she had heard
Showed us she should not exist
She is too close to a modern witch
We condemned her in a cat fight
For being as sly as a wily fox
The slur digs deep and goes far
Into the ridges of her heart's radius
Where it challenges her mixed ethos
Hurting her as intended is obvious
So it promotes a natural prejudice
Knowing she heard the hatred of the herd
It hit the target of her heart
As was the aim of each tainted word

No need to philosophize
We can use hate as lies
Sticks and stones may well break bones
Yet words are the wounds we reap
Years later words still make us weep
Words stay as a loan we always own
Knowing every day we can never repay

Comparing her to any animal
Places her value as minimal
Making the hidden hurt subliminal
Using a curse to denounce her as worse
Than every average valueless animal
Strikes as hard as their blood seeps
For with a swish the wounded wish
Reserved for them on a scrapheap
Condemning BLM while denying ALM
Forever cuts and hurts her scalpel deep

A Claim to a Name

It may well be that
Man gave names to all the animals
Whether they were in a cage or the jungle or a kennel
And whether they turned out to be a cat or a camel
And named after a cigarette or the choppy Channel
But those points flow a bit close to the master
Taking advantage of a natural human disaster
Of the Massa to rename a slave
The captives of war or our trade
For whom the price was paid
In the links of a clanking chain
On being the vanquished
Then feeling the victor's rain
To stay in their lane
That is a continuing wrong
Whatever the raid or a fight
Given a name to make it right
Changes nothing for someone
On the outside who will never belong

So the right to call
Any other creature by a name
Is a claim that fixes and forms and tames
By those who forge the game and frame
When morality falls to slumber
The gain of that hidden rain
Outweighs the captive's pain

As each creature becomes a number
Marginal forever as a forever criminal
The ID photo by us as nature's police
Make them the victims of our caprice
Devoid of choice and voice
A slave with an unpaid invoice
The Massa with his whip
Lash-on-lash on each hip
Held in check with a halter
So their freedom never falters
As we fleece goose-grease and geese
We are their forever Massa
Incarnate slavers as their mouthpiece

The Pangolin's Saviour

Who cares if it is one more pangolin
Caught by a slice of the poacher's machete
Catching each scale with skin on skin
Dirty hands and sour heart so hot and sweaty

Who cares about one more pangolin
Killed in the rush of the poacher's crush
For the prize of their scales as medicine
Then left to die in agony alone in the bush

Who cares if it is one more pangolin
The most poached mammal on earth
It is hardly a crime or even a sin
Catching a creature for cash shows its worth

Who cares if it is one more pangolin
If it satisfies our never-ending vanity
Destined for the bin we rescued our kin
If not imagine what their fate would be

If we failed to rescue them
Think about their destiny
Dying in the wild in nature's misery
Far from being questionable behaviour
We are doing them all a favour
In killing them we are their saviour

They have been here 65 million years
There is no reason for crocodile tears
Living on our peopled planet
We are hardly a gannet
By eating their fleshy meat
Their scales as our medicine
Their blood as an aphrodisiac
Is hardly the act of an ego-maniac

The Price of a Pangolin

May you find that your scales
Will weigh in the seat of justice
Each one being a winding trail
Balanced against our Judas kiss

What is wrong with the pangolin
That we cannot take them in
Much as when the world began
We claim it was solely for man

For wherever we live
For them our world
Is where they are hurled
So our lives can pan out as planned
One more Wuhan is where we stand

For then with the pangolin's death
We can all breathe easily
Each has taken their last breath
For all in our world to see

Or is it the unjust impostor
That is visible in all of us
We stalk the jungle as a mass killer
Devoid of any feeling and no fuss

What is special about the pangolin
That we cannot use its skin
When their death gives us breath
Our best defence to a cruel coincidence
Their scales pales into insignificance
Balanced against being our medicine
The price of their life
Balanced against our need for sex
Is outweighed in so many ways
Sucked and swallowed by our vortex

Since 2000 a million have been massacred
They are the world's most traffic wild animal
Yet the world wants to ban friendly poachers
When it is only one more to trap and trammel

Your wish for to live a long life
Reflect the truth on your tongue
So you can roll in your jack-knife
To stay strong and mighty young
Then to wander in the wild
As you have always done
Avoiding the heads so defiled
Spend your days in the setting sun
May you find a peace you deserve
Then breathe in free and fine air
Keep your centre on the curve
Though in a world that does not care

You will only prise from our vice
What you need to be freed
From our dream and your nightmare
By the scales of law and a real prayer

A Zoonotic Reservoir

Follow the zoonotic river
From an animal reservoir
That flows and grows in the ruin
That drew in
Every creature
That flew in
The air around Wuhan
That grew in
The water around Wuhan
They slew in
The fields around Wuhan
Where the crew in
The Virology Institute
Avoid the truth by a mute response
To the question everyone wants
To know
Which they rue in
And let the world
Stew in
While the river stills flows
While the sludge grows
While the reservoir cries
While the river still dies
While the wildlife
Brew in
While the world sleeps
While the world weeps
Tears with no limit in size
Martyrdom versus our panjandrum
Beneath the barbaric Beijing skies

Food for Thought

Lizzie said to Maggie
As old friends often do
I've been thinking lately
About those nasty foreigners
Who are cruel through and through
I've been thinking lately
About animals and what
Those lousy foreigners do.

Maggie nodded and smiled
The way people often do
Listening all the while to Lizzie
Never doubting what was true

You know those lousy foreigners
They will eat anything that moves
It does not matter what it is
They will eat claws and hooves

You know those lousy foreigners
They will eat the eyes of a fish
They will eat the soul of a sole
Straight from the dish if it is fresh

You know those lousy foreigners
They will eat a bat or even a rat
Make sure you keep your mog hidden
Because they will even eat your cat

You know those lousy foreigners
And it is not just your little mog
You have to watch them hawk-style
They will steal and then eat your dog

You know those lousy foreigners
There is something even worse
So keep your stable door closed
Because they will even eat your horse

The Maggie said to Lizzie
Let's forget about the foreigners' habits
And the world those cannibals inhabit
What do you fancy to eat?

I've got something so sweet
It will be a real treat.
I've got a chicken in the kitchen
And part of a heart of a cow
And a calf with neat sweet feet
That would be hard to beat
But if you don't fancy any of that
I promise your hunger will be slaked
I've got a huge hunk of steak
That will make your palate drool
As I always think as a rule
I imagine you'll agree with me
A meal is not a meal
Without lashings of gravy
On a plate piled high with meat

Lizzie licked her lips
And gently massaged her hips
Don't you agree? Maggie said
Seeing the body on the bed of bread
As her gaping mouth clamped upon
The juicy fresh dead fried head

Let's all go to the Zoo

The people are all happy
The children are so glad
The wonderful thing so snappy
Is no one has any reason to be sad

We're all going to the zoo
How about you?

Zoos are such fine places
With all those seeking shiny faces
And nothing but education it traces
People trade glances as the tiger paces

We're all going to the zoo
How about you?

Yet for those with another vision
See through eyes something so true
From the inside there is a collision
By a group of our caged denizens
Serving time for no crime in our prison
A confused feeling has long since risen
With closed eyes she shared their view
For them our world is a kangaroo zoo

We're all leaving the zoo
How about you?
Eyeball-to-eyeball connected
Meeting the unspoken question
Silence followed the silence
No answer to the suggestion
Are you coming too?

Job's Cat

Sam Spurns was walking through the park on the way to an important interview for a job she had coveted for a long time. It was not any old boring job, but a creative one that would allow her to be herself in approach and quality and style. The job would reflect her character as Spurns was a lady who brooked no dissent and took no prisoners.

As she was on her journey she suddenly heard a mewling cry from the bushes. She stopped in her tracks. She went into the bushes and saw, crouching in the corner, a tiny black and white whimpering wasted kitten.

She stroked the kitten. She picked her up and held her. She held her close to her chest. The kitten was shivering. The kitten stopped crying. The kitten started to quietly purr. As she stroked her the kitten's purr had its own gentle rhythm.

She looked at her watch. Time was tight and fleeting with swiftness as the interview appointment loomed large in her mind. In that instant she figured the two competing interests: does she just abandon the kitten to her future in the hope that someone else will rescue the creature? Does she place the kitten back in the bush and rush off to try and get the job of her dreams?

She was in swaying through ping-pong emotions as the proprioceptors battled through her heart and mind towards her centric soul.

Although it was only about 30 seconds the choice was clear and direct: does she forget about the kitten or forget about the job?

She decided that was no choice at all.

She went to the interview.

She took the kitten with her.

She explained to the interviewers what had happened on her journey and why she attended with the kitten.

The interviewers conducted the interview while the kitten gently and quietly slept inside her coat, close to her own beating heart.

At the end the interviewers told her that normally they saw every candidate, checked the references and had a second interview.

However by bringing the kitten to the interview which could have been to her detriment, she showed her true character.

They offered her the job on the spot.

She accepted. She agreed to start the following week.

Besides being a resounding success, there was one other point that swayed the interviewers. At the end when they asked her the interview-type question, 'Do you have any questions you'd like to ask us?' She answered plaintively, 'Only one, can I bring the kitten to work?'

'I don't know if she's microchipped or not and if so, will be able to be traced. Though I doubt it. I suspect as she's so frail and emaciated and thin, she was just dumped just discarded like the Christmas puppy with the ripped paper from the broken presents. If I can't get anyone else to take her, can she come with me?'

To her surprise, then as now, they said 'Yes.' She always figured that 'Don't ask don't get as the best approach.' Now it proved to be the case.

Anyway she did exactly that and the kitten, named Ida B. after the great lady herself who was her silent mentor, became the mascot of the office. She was named and pictured on the 'paper' as a logo. She was a talking point for each new contract and project which both broke the ice and was a reflection on the company's principles.

Ida B. is based on a true case where the crème of the crème prevailed while Spurns and Ida B. were the cats who got the cream. The Interviewers told Sam they gave her the Job because she passed their personal test: "Be the person your cat thinks you are."

The Fish that failed to Scream

He threw the line that fooled the fish
The rusty hook caught the bream
He could hardly see her struggle
Part of the joy of his serene dream
As he overcame her strength
By the rising line and his length
Catching her silver scale in the stream
He was secretly glad fish do not scream

The bent hook curled around her throat
The time was right for his lucky strike
Close on the surface he grabbed her
The prize was a splashing thrashing pike
He found her fight added to the delight
Using his power and all his might
Catching her silver scale in the stream
He was secretly glad fish do not scream

He threw the lasso into the river
Intent on catching a another carp
His jagged hook and line and sinker
Reflected his mind blunt and sharp
Like the last throw of a cardsharp
Wanting to make sure he got that carp
Catching her silver scale in the stream
He was secretly glad fish do not scream

Intending on ending with a perky perch
He stood close to the fast water's ledge
His line got caught in a drooping birch
That dragged him to the snagged edge
Losing balance he slipped on the bank
A crooked hook in his tongue as he sank
Angler and line swinging in the stream
Both gripped beneath the vice slipstream

Beneath the water open-mouthed
Bubbles killed his fish-like shout
The perch was dragged down and out
While the angler was dragged all about
The spreading pain shot through him
His life flashed in a nightmare scheme
Echoed by his heart-rending scream
Followed by scream-after-scream

In that moment he lost all doubt
About the cold-fish-no-pain shout
The angler so often used to spout
A different time and a different theme
Drowned as if he was another bream
Sinking as no one heard his stifled scream
Like catching her silver scale in the stream
His heart went boom-boom-boom
Seeing the crashing flashing watery tomb
No longer secretly glad fish do not scream

The Palace of Plunder Land

Using a strange sign language he asked
'What have I done to deserve such a fate?'
As another inmate lined up
When the tiger opened the gate

Then the next in line asked
'Why am I locked inside this cage?'
As she was assigned her task
Flying in a circling swooping rage

And then the next and the next
Engaged in a weird pretext
All were lost in a pointless quest
Asking, 'Why pray are we here?
Are we to be perpetual deportees
Or shown dignity due to any guest'

For them there was no answer except
The one they could not bear to hear:
Each of you is our perpetual slave
We decide the time for your grave

For who is the jack and who is the knave
Has no meaning now you are in our power
Get used to the shock of your status as a slave
Now your world is ours every hour-on-hour

You will have to get used to the scene
You have an inside view of a human zoo
You have the picture that makes us richer
You are the prized part of our barbecue

A Whale of a Time

When you take the life of a whale
With a strike that explodes inside
You can feel his pain in Braille
When you see that spouting fountain
And the magic of that sea mountain
As he glides through the ocean
And you get the shared notion
To follow where he leads
And make sure he bleeds
Beneath the beauty of a cold moon
Only darkened by the boon
Of a hot hammered harpoon

Do not blame me I am only the captain
I just follow orders
Across all the borders

Sweeping the seven seas
Doing what others ask of me
When I set sail
I risk the gale
Out on the trail
Follow their wail
There is no avail
Of their travail
I am here to deliver a whale

Do not blame me I am only a sailor
Trying to make a living
Taking all that the whale's giving
A modern Jack Tar it is true
Doing what I am told to do
We cannot afford to fail
We are there just to nail
His flashing tail
The real tell-tale
I will assail
Of their travail
I am here to deliver the whale

Do not blame me I am only a buyer
Looking for a profit
How much I can make off it
When the competition is rife
Letting them make a good life
They are just part of the retail

When their weapons impale
The capture of the whale
No more bail
Monitor the flail
Of their travail
I am here to deliver the whale

Do not blame me I am only the customer
Wanting another tasty meal
At a price that is the best deal
His death gives me hope
As I love soap on a rope
The smell I have to inhale
I do not want it stale
Or their gaol
Only the sale
With no bail
Of their travail
I am here to devour the whale

Together we have all aided
Economies we have braided
Then there is the side-line
When the whale is mine
And the wails of the whales
No reason for blackmail
No different than a foxtail
It is off the scale
Getting a giant male

Draw the veil
Of their travail
We are here to deliver the whale

Catching him sharpens our soul jaded by life
We do not fuss too much about any wildlife
We just trust in the thrust of our explosive knife

You are looking at it
From the wrong direction
We do it from pure affection
See the swishing tail
Hear her bellowing wail
As the harpoon explodes
Our heads are in overload
If it is female
If it is frail
We do not quail
Of their travail
We are here to deliver the whale

You have to understand
That at sea or on land
Everything changes and rearranges
For you and me our destiny is planned
After all he has had his time
It is now time to call it quits
He has lived in our shadow

For far too long
And we are here
To make sure his inside splits
We catch them when the sea sprays their wine
That is why we caught him in his peak-prime
Everyone has a whale of a time
It is not as if we commit a crime
The rhythm of the seas is our rhyme
After all until the moment she is caught
Even the whale has a great time
Like a lover in life's race
She too enjoys the chase
You should see her smiling face
She knows there is no escape
From the whaler's intent to rape
We take her out in a bloody blaze
A smile a harpoon could not erase

Without a wish to cause them any strife
It is a natural part of them being wildlife
Their price for living is paid by our knife

So shake the dice and toss a coin
We will decide which one to purloin
Hold tight and gird your loin
You might get the chance to join

When you are a giant among men
It is a thrill when we wreak our will
A thrill we share when we kill
There is no fancy word to add to a frill
Much like your pet with his prey
Getting her in our grip makes our day
That is a bill that is always a winterkill
Truth's tart pill is best told by the shrill
Of the lone whippoorwill
Believe me there is no substitute
For the fire inside when you shoot
Is our gain as her pain is mute
We are intent on stealing her loot
 We all walk tall wearing a jackboot

The fat cat lab Rat

Who wants to wear a wig or a hat
When it is so much easier to kill a rat
To the background wail of Fake Fat
A cure for baldness is where it's at

Forget the fact we are all obese
Feeding our faces with midnight feasts
Any reason we can use we will seize
While the growing rodent bodies freeze

We do not care what you allege
We are all living life on the ledge
Drinking to excess takes us to the edge
A daily promise to take the pledge
Instead forget a feckless promise
A rat's life is the thick end of our wedge

We all snort the snow white horse
Lawyers and lovers sharing each curse
Junkies in alleys shoot up with force
Kill a million rats as a matter of course

We can do what we like as it is only a rat
The same as choking a mangy stray cat
Or eating a pangolin or a wild captive bat
Experiment on anything all day in the lab
The place for another bat and cat and rat
Put them up with the pigs then rat-a-tat-tat

We poison them as our tasters
To protect us as greedy wasters
Lest we get fatter is all that matters
Get the gat so their insides go splat
Bullets or gas or listening to Fake Fat
Anything as long as we do not get fat

On the Rack

The suffragette burned with a passion
That was outweighed by compassion
Without a care for the ideas in fashion
She figured that vivisection was false
Learned from an 'English Hungers' waltz
The sold science was total schmalz
So a bunch of Stag-spanner sabs
Burgled the locked experimental lab
Grabbed the scientists who dished
Death's rewards to their exhibits
Representing their mantra wish
As a daily chant to gain a grant
While the exhibits were unable to move
Used to prove the academic conundrum:
Whether rape is sexual or borne of power
Everyone knew the cue was pure bunkum

Sabs used their power at the midnight hour
They grabbed and placed in the same space
Science had reserved for the two chimps
By the state-aided academic pair of pimps
Their pale bodies shrunk into a deadly limp
Then the scientists performed the same task
When the pain and pressure pierced their minds
They did not have to look too far to find
The answer to their question about power or sex
As the force of the sabs was set to destroy them
Proved the practice was no less than a human hex

They wondered as they felt the fire
Though they tried to hide their pain
Using a mental state on their loss and gain
Both died wondering whether with Kant:
If we survive could we use our daily chant
To trail our holy grail to gain one last grant
Then subject truth to a scientific transplant?

Mouse-proof Science

With a feeling colder than Arctic ice
The white-coated scientist loaded the dice
Grabbed another batch to splice
Inject them with their nasty spice
So many they appear as grains of rice
Lined up as another sacrifice
To find a cure for very kind of lice
And every kind of human vice
Complete each exercise at least twice
And then repeat it in a thrice
Blind and deafen and their limbs ready to slice
By taking the scientific community advice
Always calculated and opaque and concise
Strap them in a metal device
Whatever you do avoid being over-nice

After all the doped-up hordes
Are only a bunch of miniature rats
Or being even more precise
Paying the price of being mice
On their one-way journey
As they travel to the land of endless Nod
While we are vivisectionists playing God
So we can send them to a science paradise

It is easy to say about a chimpanzee
That they are 98.8% the same as you and me
You could even say the same about a donkey
But we can do whatever we want to mice
Because the public are unlike Hermann
Who eulogised a mouse who was his friend
While they see mice as a form of vermin
Mice are not worth the candle
They are not even worth the wick
So they get their kicks
Failing to kick against the pricks

Stopcock and Bull

The crowd looks and waits
Their eyes fixed on the gate
Then it is flung open
So the huge bull escapes
Towards the sawdust Caesars
Naked Emperor plays Macbeth
So he charges towards the capes
But only towards his own death

The crowd waits with bated breath
Nostrils flaring ready for their fun
As they wait for him to bake
Beneath the burning cruel crisp sun
Counting the time it will take
Before he takes his very last breath

The cuadrilla removed his horns
To even up the odds in the fight
When the matador stabbed him
Knowing he was out of luck
With no horns to prick and hook
A coward with a ready-made victim

The picador parades around the arena
Tiptoes as a prancing ballerina
When he thrusts the sharpened darts
All around her fear-beating heart
Her cries make the crowd meaner
Laughing as she is their misdemeanour
The delirious crowd as a mass of hyenas

The matador catches the mood of the crowd
All their laughter and shouts echo so loud
Waiting for the spreading pool-spilled blood
Dancing with his dagger drawn in an ego-cloud

A bull bleeds in the sun-kissed run
As always it is a one-sided pendulum
So each one's life will be undone
Where the weight swings against the bull
Where hearts are vacant and minds are full
Of hate and pride in a bitter sour skull

Each one in the crowd
Each one with the sword
Finds a thrill in a cheap kill
While their hate is heard
Taking a life by cheaper words

The priests clapped and laughed
For too long and too loud
Locked in pride in a shroud
Until their hands bled with shame
Although they knew no one said
Their pained blood was the same
Shade as that that the bull shed

At Communion the next morning
Though there was no mourning
For it was and is only a bull
For the priest knows the prayers
He offers on the body and bread
Shared with such feeling
The thoughts still reeling
Through his muddled head
When he claps and claps
In every bull fight
Every day and night
His excuse another religious ruse
Being finally a bunch of bull Shiite
The priest looked at his hands
Saw the stigmata of the blood

Of every bull that he saw
Being tortured to death
His malice in his chalice
Struck him hard with a thud
He knew with conviction
He witnessed a crucifixion

The cuadrillas wander so proud
Applauded by the baying crowd
The subalteros dressed in silver
But the matador is clothed in gold
He grabs her ears and tail as trophies
An echo of the foxhunting landscape
For the same reason as fruits of rape

The cry from the crowd is so loud
Every word can be heard
As a repeated crescendo 'Kill her!'
The torture is dressed up as culture
Proving why 'matador' means 'killer'
Then the English tourists all go home

From the start the method and the mood
Is to steal her heart and create a feud
Anything as long as the crowd is intrigued
And to make the odds even she was fatigued
Her weakness reflects the banderillo's strength
Plunging the darts into her
To dial into the crowd's wavelength

Then the picador begins to prance
And drives a lance into her
To satisfy the growing crowd
Of poseurs and voyeurs
Impatient for torture to recur
As the matador performs
With the frightened hooded
Snorting blindfolded horse
Dancing in the sand
With a handy harpoon in his hand
He drives it into her with so much force
The bull bellows and starts to collapse
And the matador jumps down and laughs
In time with the laughter and clamour
As the crowd waits
Impatient for death's dull glamour
While ever-hungry they clap and clap
The matador gives her one last angry slap
Her last gasp as she tries hard to rise
Then sinks and dies before their flint eyes

It is not a question of being squeamish
While the money pours into their coffers
From tourists who follow culture's offer
They gain from the English on arriving
Who tell tales on their roam back home
Glorify the sunshine in the English rain
While their taxes pays for the bulls' pain
Buying death is a pleasure
They learn to treasure
As a spectacle of leisure

Yet they dwell on the hate
Without any hope
When against their wish
If not their bulging purse
Yet when they say they find it perverse
Seeing a glimpse of their own hearse
They are intent not to discover
A truth as rare as an Eskimo in the Sahara
A truth hid by panda-ringed mascara
Proof of the ever phoney history trope
The English are a nation of animal lovers

Jonah in Pamplona

Hemingway was a cruel fool
Who as a rule loved violence
As long as it affected someone else
Until one day he reached past the pelts
Then grabbed his shotgun
To clean his teeth and brains
One last time so nothing
But his raddled remains remained

Their hero and the hooded horse
Caught in the snare and trapped
Where misery meets morality
Forgotten as they are mapped
Confined in the crowd's memory

Jonah moved from Arizona to Pamplona
Besotted by the running in the corridor
Though he loved the gunning more
He would go anywhere
As long as he would find there
Some kind of death in the afternoon
A helpless defenceless animal's demise
Their date with fate never came too soon
As their agony always sparked his eyes alive

Hemingway was the classic abuser
Who regaled in the glory of the loser
Always being the first accuser
Of anyone who dared to criticise
The plain cruelty before his eyes
As the sight of a smoking gun
Made his cold blood start to run
Faster than the bull weighing a ton
Killing for him was freedom and fun
Killing was the rhythm of his mind
When death arrived he came alive
Except that is for the last time

A Canterbury Story

Chaucer told a worthy tale
Of a cock and a certain ruse
That Hemingway would often use
An ego that only praise would sate
And an appetite for animal abuse
That could not wait
As he found the flood
Of someone else's blood
Would make his heart beat
Just a little faster
And so it is no disaster
And equally as a blaster
It is no surprise his own demise
Came from a ritual borne
Of the scorching mid-day sun
But ratcheted up to at least a ton
He hoped the killing of a bull
Would not be limited to one

With that optimistic thought
He had no time for a wreathe
When he brushed his teeth
With a sawn-off shotgun

His faithful dog pawed at the bathroom door
Until the hinges could not hold it any more
Broke in and waited by his master on the floor
Yet love is not the way of Hemingway
Who only found personal glory
In his bitter souped up story
Of killing for killing's sake
But listen and perhaps learn
A lesson of what is true
Perhaps in his own way
Hemingway is no different
Than me and you

Bull-at-a-Gate

The jaundiced Judge
Chanced upon a judgement
He had to give that was to decide
Whether the matador or picador or toreador
Should die or live as a tradition
Whether he could override
The bare fact it raised so much tax
With the ingrained abuse side-by-side
Should he aid its timely abolition

The Judge attacked it head-on
Asking the Counsel in a voice-weary tone
Borne of a sleepless long-lost night
Is the question no less than whether a bullfight
Is part of culture and a sport or just animal abuse
And so can never be right?

And anyway who can tell
Who has the right to sell
Another life or line or lie
About who has fallen on the racecourse
Who objects to eating a knackered horse
When fishing and shooting just rocks
Is no different to killing a fox
Or a stag or hanging a bull
On a production-line hook
Or research in a science book
From an experiment
Is it just another way
For an academic on a frolic
Using language that is hyperbolic
Finding a fun way to pay the rent?

The Judge waited for an answer to appear
A deep thinker he was known to be swift
Yet Counsel stayed silent then quite quietly said
'I figure on this one I'll take the Fifth.'

The Judge could see through his scheme
He said that is American legalese
Use English logic and law if you please
So the Counsel grabbed his gown
He figured it was time for prudence
He shot a quizzical look at the Judge
And said I'll exercise my right of silence

A Crush on the Movies

To call her sick is far from enough
To call her evil is not rough enough
To call her obtuse does not begin to grapple
The sour apples hanging in her empty chapel
Whose sermon only delivered its hate
Untimely and as usual a laced bait

She smiled while the kitten took its last breath
As her high heels crushed the kitten to death
Then she put her hipster clothes back on
Collected her money saying 'see you honey'
To the pervert making the film in colour
To match the model and make it fuller

When the machine screeched into the night
Making copy-on-copy that would soon take flight
Among the perverts and paedophiles whose smiles
At the killing of a kitten crushed in a sleaze push
Would provide a rush until the next killing slush
Would satisfy their soiled spoiled porno wiles

Aided and abetted by a woman too crass to realise
She was Jim Crow revisited whatever was her pay
She was a rainbow shadow of the modern KKK

Has she forgotten the Tulsa Massacre in 1921
A century later the same gun was used in 2021
Has she forgotten the body of Adam Toledo
Killed by a cop as just one more 'so-so'
Has she forgotten the body of Daute Wright
Cut down in his prime in broad daylight
Has she seen a reflection of her own deception
Where in the scales of what is black and white
No in-between pose if truth is forced out of sight
One act is always wrong and one is always right

She fondles the wad of cold used cash
The price of a life she stole
Counting each note of the whole
What she has won and lost on the lash
The mathematics of her misery
Is plain for all to see
Her gain in filling a sadist's role
She counts the cost to her sold-out soul

Just like *The Zong* of her drowned ancestors
Just like the history of her past still festers
Just like Martha White saw black was right
Just like the peddler who is vice-bitten
Just like her pornographic heart is written
Just like her being rose-tinted dollar-smitten
Just like failing to be a frontline protester
Just like being another Massa molester
Just like stiletto heels in her coloured skeleton
Just like killing a defenceless piebald kitten

She has crushed the skin of her history
She has pushed the Jim Crow memory

Life is for the Dying

Being part of the killing
Of a creature you can feature
In stories of glory
About the chase and the face
Of the fox whose sly look
Shows Charlie has got a lot of pluck
Until we charge down with 40 hounds
To remove that grin from his smug mug
And as the first hound
Drags him down to the ground
And the second and third follow
And find they are joined by the other 37
That is our idea of heaven
With thundering hooves and claws
Which rip the fox from limb to limb
We hack off his head and tail
A sight that never fails to excite
Touches parts no other thrill will reach

Makes for a bullyrag jokey speech
About their blood-filled screech
As easy as squashing a ripe peach
We never care about their plight
Never haunts our Hunt Ball night

Our thrill splits the countryside
As our alliance is our science
For the bites show he has no fight
When he is outnumbered by 40 to one
Throwing him beneath our blunderbuss
So each conscience is swiftly concussed

Oh yes we showed that wily fox
We do not box and cox
We took him out and snuffed his shout
We are the boss
His life is no loss
At least to any of us
He is vermin and just our pus

Because we sure as hell showed the fox
When the teeth of 40 hounds locks
On your throat you have nowhere
On earth left to hide and run
Except towards our terrier man's gun
Except towards our man-made hell

Yet somewhere in the distance
There is an old school bell
That chimes to mark out the time
Of their sell as another kind of cell

Politicians mounted their steeds
To revive their country culture
Sharing making the fox a carrion
Politico prejudice their vulture clarion

Where animals are concerned
A lesson we have learned
Avoid the one whose tongue
Is heaped high with rust
One type you can trust
Less than a politician
Springing from the same stem
Is when there are two of them
Then they can double the means to evade
When their falsehood is ready-made
They are as honest as a sundial in the shade

We do not care for the drag
We do not care for the law
A fox or hare or a stag
We will smash the badger's jaw
We will snap and break their paw
We kill whoever loses our draw
We thrill seeing death in the raw

The 21st Century Treblinka

Do you hate the Nazis
With their cruel passion
Do you hate the Nazis
Devoid of all compassion

Do you hate the Nazis
Whose abuse has no ration
Do you hate the Nazis
Seeing victims cold and ashen

Then both near and far
Think about their mirror
Whether or not in uniform
It was shaped and deformed
On their creed of cruelty
Whether far or near
Reflected in their mirror
Whether far or near
It was their chance to preen
On a face each must have seen

Do you hate the Nazis
Whose instinct was to kill
Do you hate the Nazis
Destroying each stranger's will

Do you hate the Nazis
Ovens they intended to fill
Do you hate the Nazis
Murder their practised skill

Do you hate the Nazis
Who were common criminals
Do you hate the Nazis
Valued people below animals

It made Isaac Singer see the sight
And hear the woeful sound
Of their frightened flight
And their hearts start to pound
Nostrils twitching at an awful smell
Only the toughest victim could tell
Then delivered the eternal stinker
That damned every clinker
Damned every head shrinker
The truth on removing his blinker
Made Isaac a prophet and a thinker:
To animals we are all Nazi's
And for them it's an eternal Treblinka

Cattle packed like sardines in cattle trucks
Lined up in a clanking chained queue
Among the remains of their stomachs
Splashing through the mud and muck
Prodded and stunned by electric guns

Bleeding from every forced orifice
Bleeding from fear while speechless
We all choose to forget our trespass
Only remembering what we tasted before
So our open palate and closed heart
Clamours for more and more and more

Our modern concentration camp
Is a version of a new Ravensbruck
Our modern factory farm
Is designed purely to harm
The inmates that enter the gates
For whom only torture awaits
No one cares and no one grieves
No one who enters ever leaves
Crowded closer than herrings in a tin
Caught between a crime and a sin
Line-by-line with no escape from fate
Our daily dose of animal morphine
Our factory farm starts with a cow
Or a lamb or a pig or a sheep
Whose bits and giblets we reap
Replacing a feigned culture with torture
While our victims thrash and die in a heap

Are the English and Faroese and Japanese
Mere doppelgangers of the Germans
Seeing them as the same species
No different to the others you see

Especially those we foster
Particularly those impostors
Whose masks hide you from me
Morally we know we are pygmies
For animals we are all Nazis
A factory farm our jackboot arm
A creation for those creatures
Their death our favourite feature
All we learn from those teachers
While living in the our global Ritz
As their body shatters and mind splits
In our world as an Animals' Auschwitz

Zuckerberg's Judas Goat

Zuckerberg boasts about how he digs
Eating his freshly-killed pig
And how he kills a goat
Because he is behind a moat
He figures it is fine to slit the throat
Of a pig and a goat
To end the life of an animal
Too weak to resist
The billionaire butcher's kiss
When the knife twists
In his clenched fist
Yet Zuckerberg is no sectarian
As his property is not pelf:
'I've basically become a vegetarian
Since the only meat I'm eating
Is from animals I've killed myself.'

Except the pig and goat
Cannot speak or reveal
But as both can feel
Neither can they reveal
Fear captured in their last squeal

Who says their last squeal
Was not telling Zuckerberg
Revisit the address at Gettysburg
Or death-row fear of Rosenberg
Zucker has ideas as cold as a fridge
That holds the pig
Before he holds her on his bridge
Though words float across his brow
Their meaning escape him for now
Given that his mind is never stationary
For a start he would be smart
To invest in a school dictionary
Zucker could look up 'vegetarian'
Then his mind might meet his heart

With my bow and Arrow

It is such a bore
And a chore for some hairy boar
To have to be removed from the groove
Of the huertas which smell so sweet
And are even better to eat
So when the wild art creatures
Are denied food to live
When after all the huertas are ours
Taking hours to cultivate so your mouth
Has to go south
It is for the best that they all go west
As the hunters with a bow and arrow
So the point hits the vein
And all that remains is the rain
If the spattered black blood
And of course the unremitting pain
When the hunter fails in his aim
When he succeeds
The smell of blood
Causes the other boars to flee as to stay
Invites an arrow as they eat a marrow
And are despatched where they stand
Though hunting in England
By the bow is now banned
Because it is too cruel
So it is better it is used there
Where except for the bores in Parliament
The real ones are not shot where they stand
Content to hide outside the pain
As modern-day replicas of faked-eyed Petain

Equally it is little wonder such an enterprise
Is followed by a clown in camouflage
Who has the dazed mind and blank eyes
And a heart as cold as a Titanic iceberg
Appealing to the frozen soul of Zuckerberg
Seeking the truffle finding boar
As Zucker is a sucker for tucker
Maybe he will meet a man with a mirror

When Zucker meets his mucker
And tucks into his tucker
Hears the rhymes of changing times
When the death bell chimes
With no reason to fumble
As his loaded poised rifle
Moves from goat to pig to boar
He should stand close to the mirror
Then Zucker will instantly recognise
Which animal is the Pulitzer prize bore

The Seal of a Suffragette

Gertrude Ansell took up the cudgel
For those held under the thumb
By those who had become
Masters at the table dropping breadcrumbs
Holders of the key and masters of the fate
Keeping animals and women outside the gate
Except when awaiting their fate inside the gate
Of the man-made prison to be force-fed to death
Of a vivisection lab for a science shibboleth

Mary Clarke was the mistress of protest
Who smashed the State's secret armour
She figured that was meant to harm her
And the women and animals too

As she flew into their political nest
As ever as an unwanted guest
Full of life and too much zest
Yet she was bound to lose the contest
When the guards placed her under arrest

They lined her up and held her down
Her arms and legs strapped tight
Forced her neck to catch the light
Forced her head to hang up right
Her body primed so she could swallow
Her mind ready for their kind of gallows
To them she was just another dogsbody
Then they poured the food inside her body
Just another busybody who was nobody
Who counted for nothing with anybody
They filled the tube right to the brim
And poured and poured every last drop
So nothing was wasted as their grip
Held her neck as tight as a noose
They needed no excuse for their abuse
When Mary Clarke became a human goose

Mary was one more suffragette
They would choose to soon forget
Strike her down without any regret
When the water and the gruel was fed
By force to destroy her liver and head
Poured and poured until they were sure
Mary was deader than a Dodo is dead

Silence of Science

Without research there would be no vaccine
It is essential we use research as our routine
The vaccine is the answer to the pandemic
If it means sacrificing a few million animals
Well rest assured that is purely academic
As for saying that our abuse of animals
Is the reason we created the pandemic
Well that is an idle misguided polemic
Like a burglar blaming the bank
For holding too much cash
When the disease is merely a backlash
Against our dash to treat animals as trash

Yet two questions continue to cause us congestion:
If animals are the same as us
What is our moral answer to causing them pain?
If animals are different to us
What is our moral purpose in causing them pain?
It seems that maybe the law
Is meant to protect the vulnerable
Yet when it came to slaves
The law found it to be tolerable
Century-upon-century make it comparable
But the law still finds the justice question
Equally easy to ignore as if it was unanswerable

Yet the answer to our quest
For a cure for every disease
Is to vivisect a million victims
Too vulnerable to resist
Why forfeit a gift of a monkey or a horse
When follow Mengele is our best course
And try another experiment
On things we own too weak to prevent
An injected needle of death as our intent
While our crooked silent science need
Catches the concentration camp creed
Where our morality is hooked and bent

The Lawyer loved lager and Lime

A llama walked into the Queen's Retreat.
He ordered a lager and lime.
The barman was somewhat surprised.
He tried to engage him in a conversation.
I've not seen you in here before. Are you local?
No, I'm just here for a month or so.
I see. What do you do?
I'm a lawyer. I'm a consultant for that new factory across the road. I advise on the health and safety legislation.
The llama was not very interested in talking.
He took his pint and went to a table in the corner.
The llama takes out a huge book and flicks through it. Periodically he reads a passage and makes notes on a yellow pad.
The barman is intrigued and keeps him in his vision.
After about an hour he gets up, closes his briefcase and leaves the pub.
He waves to the barman who waves back.
Day after day, week in and week out, the llama visits the pub and orders a lager and lime.
Not many of our customers drink that. You seem to like it a lot?
I love it, son. Tell you the truth lager and lime is the juice of the gods. Before I started drinking it I was as bald as a snooker ball. Now look at me? I've got more hair that the average Yeti.
Well, I can't argue with that.

One day the llama visited the pub and told the barman he would be moving out of the area in a few days.

Why is that? he asked, as they had become friendly.

My contract will expire. I'll be moving to a new post.

Shortly after he left that day, the ringmaster of a visiting circus visited the pub.

Would you mind if I put up a few posters?

No, go right ahead.

I'll do anything to get a few more bums on seats.

Well, I have someone who might be useful to you.

Who? Tell me more. I'm all ears.

He told him about the llama and his habits.

The ringmaster listened intently. At the end he said, yes I would really like to meet him. From what you say I reckon our punters would love him. Would you do me a favour?

Yes, of course. What did you have in mind?

Here's my card. Would you give it to him next time you see him? Ask him to get in touch?

I'll be glad to do so.

The next day the llama visits the pub.

He orders his lager and lime and sits at the table.

The barman can hardly contain his excitement.

He hands the ringmaster's card to the llama.

This is about a circus, he says and looks a little quizzical.

'Yes. Great news. Just up your street. The ringmaster reckons he might have a job for you.

A circus?

Yes. Great isn't it?

Isn't that where all the main performers live in caravans?

That's right.

And the animals live in cages?

That's right.

And the animals are trained to do tricks for people?

That's right.

And they are hit and kicked and whipped?

Only if they are aggressive like.

And they perform in a draughty tent?

That's right.

I see.

So what do you reckon? The ringmaster is dead keen to meet you.

I'm a bit confused.

Why? What shall I tell him when I see him again?

I'm still confused.

How? Can I help at all?

Yes. Why does a ringmaster of a circus want a consultant contract lawyer?

A Trophy for Vanity

Proudly she stands with her foot
On the head of her prey
Her weapon across her shoulder
The trophy for a well-paid day
A handsome reward for the risk
She takes on every shoot
For the victim could fight back
And deprive her of the loot
She smiles so the photograph
Will capture the unleashed iron
That coursed through her
When she sees her bagged lioness
Or better still the shaggy lion
Adding another notch on her bedpost list
The feeling of power too hard to resist
Yet she fails to see through her vanity mist

The ghost of her image turned topsy-turvy
Her phoney claim to be a 'conservationist'
Cuts a tarnished symbol as some women see
The trophy hunter as naked as a naturist
The trophy hunter as nature's terrorist
The trophy killer as a stalking rapist

The rapist steals a piece of his victim
Sings his hymn of hate as a maxim
To take away as a token of his prey
To dwell on his pervert's power
Used to slay the one in the way
A perfect reminder of his crime
A mirror-image of his victim
A trophy of power that satisfies him
A rapist and trophy hunter whose vanity
Advertises a naked hatred of humanity

Sticks in your Stomach

Save your disgust as your lust for foie gras
As a delicacy tingles on your tongue
Knowing the goose whose liver you gorge
Died in agony for your palate is strong
So save your moral stance as it is as subtle
As a vegan butcher without bottle
It is time to own up as a blood-sucking leech
Hiding a blacksmith's mallet to rupture a peach

Forget criticising the French
Wrestling your conscience wrench
When you scan the menu
Knowing all too well it is true
Your palate is the pliers twisting her fate
Marked out in chalk on the blackboard slate

There is no need to translate her destiny's date
In England you can eat legal cruelty on a plate

Smell their liver and swell your belly
You can find a reason via Machiavelli
Forget the girdled goose
She just drew a deuce
Every gob is her sluice
So her taste outweighs her suffering
Given the choice it is mouth-watering
So our taste outweighs her suffering

A Colston con meets a sapient Swan

The people saw his deeds in neo-neon
Colston was a symbol of slavery as an icon
A twin combination of a monster and a moron
His grave should be visited by everyone
Who know his trader's routes and roots
Then danced upon wearing hobnail boots

A man whose ethos sailed through his crooked colon
Whose statue was hissed by a Bristol harbour swan
Glad his statue sunk quicker than a boulder
A graffiti painted hollow figure served as a trigger
For her to sit on his sagging shrugged shoulder

For a hate that was washed by scum and soon gone
The murky dock swamp showed his life as a total con
A medal pinned to his chest he could not hide
His tombstone truth serves to prove
There is no pride in genocide
No wonder the swan used his surly face to sit upon
While taking time out to wash and to preen
She noticed his thin-lipped mouth looked obscene
So she shook her feathers like a fiery tambourine
Then used his traitor's face as a ready-made latrine

Law and life and logic and Love

I know that while you were everything
In the realms of law you are just a 'thing'
Yet more than that crass legal sting
With a glance you made my heart dance
Then my soul sang with a wild zing

I know your life does not last long
I know until the end you were strong
All that was right with you
For me could never be wrong
For to me you will forever be
The lasting beauty of an unsung song

The law of life has its logic in place
One moment you are part of the race
Then you were gone as will-o'-the-wisp
My mind I find still tries to track and trace
The rare and raw beauty of your natural grace
Freedom I found in your ever-accepting face

These days you are all I ever think of
All it took was you to teach me about love
Each act as warm-hearted as a cupped dove
Inside my mind exploded in love's Molotov
As we listened to the soaring Rimsky-Korsakov
With you on my lap together we read Chekov
My hand dovetailed in your fading falling paw
Within the lasting grasp of love's locked glove

One and two and Zero

Now in the winter of some frost-ridden scene
Turned upside down so truth can hardly be seen
So different from what you might have been
Yet your invisible thread is still evergreen

While I learned from you my feline friends' collection
Is simple but complex with a shape that is convex
Without a need for magic or a moon that shone
With nothing to be lost and everything to be won

Only clear-eyed beauty goes on and on
This side of the grave your vision saved me
From the spectre of missing and musing
Always letting go of my losing and proving
It is you who braved my misery and forgave me

The eternal equation between me with you
Show the mathematics of life is untrue
Heart losing heart equals a constant rue
Always adds up to one and two and zero
When I am caught now without my hero
My natural stance against it is to be a pierrot

The law of Italian Love

The government of Italy
Have granted their citizens
A legal concession to kill seven doves
A key to the prison of hate over love

A law that takes their hard hearts
And fits as neat as a chain-mail glove
A politicians' note to catch a vote
By a show of the democracy of love

A grand stance for their citizens
Against the local flying denizens
Nothing could be better
Than being a political pacesetter

For them to be always thinking of
The lasting route towards democratic love
As neat and sweet as a Mafia blastoff
Is a mass killing of the white peace dove

Where all gangsters proliferate
At their palace of wisdom gate
Leonardo mused that regardless of purdah
Killing the babies of animals was murder

Leonardo was wise in deed and word
All he needed was his word to be heard
While his ideas on air have taken flight
On that score Leo was also right so right

Please pass the Sandwich

The women met each week
To swop a few pleasant stories
Of how their lives panned out
And all their shared past glories
They had known each other for years
Seeing each other's involuntary tears
When the animals they cared for were abused
And still held by an invisible truce
Then when no one came to claim them
On their last day they paid their way
Being put down as a spare unwanted stray

They rehearsed and repeated
Their feelings for the creatures
And all the bulletins that featured
Multiple-abuse week-in week-out

Made their blood boil and hearts shout
Abandoned and ill-treated
Every form meted and discarded as detritus
Yet they claimed they are so 'like us'

Or so they said and meant
Their words shared and never bent
They talked of hating all animal abuse
How they cared for the welfare
Of the creatures that featured
As each new batch arrived
With food and feeling
Caring and sharing their lives
With those who had no worth
Because they were cursed by birth

She hated how they were treated
As worthless wastage and baggage
Their treatment was no less than savage
The strays ending up on a one-way voyage
Then Mary said to Margaret,
'Can you please pass me a ham sandwich?'
'As it is the season of goodwill and fun
Would you prefer the turkey one?'

Fit as a butcher's Dog

The stray mongrel chanced upon the butcher
Who saw him loiter near the shop's open door
But before he became a canine burglar
The friendly butcher threw a bone on the floor

The next day the mongrel visited the butcher
And loitered again with a dog-like intent
But he had no need to become a burglar
The kindly gent gave him an open consent

Then day after day the scruffy stray
Wandered into the butcher's shop
And day after day he had a hunk of meat
And on Sunday even got a pork chop

In no time the mongrel grew strong
And almost became a watchdog
So sleek with shiny teeth and so young
He looked as fit as a butcher's dog

Far from merely being a man's best friend
This was simply a twist of pure fate
As for no reason the man had a new end
He had a feeling that was less than straight

The customers made knowing comments
That pleased the butcher somewhat
For he knew exactly what was meant
By those who wanted what he had got

So seeing the shadow of the pound signs
Illuminated by the lightning lure of greed
He grabbed the mongrel as he whined
And balanced what he believed was a need

He took the mongrel out the back
Held him and gave him a whack
Then swiftly slit its tight throat
The unnamed mongrel dead in the dark
Barely had time for his last bark
As the butcher wiped his blood on his coat

No one asked about the dog
He was just one more butcher's stray
But was now another hunk of meat
The ghost of a stray on any street any day

The butcher had a honed sense of humour
So he hung a handwritten sign outside
Saying 'Toilet-trained Dog Wanted'
And waited with the numbers on his side

They wandered towards him each passing day
There was one after another passing stray
Until one who missed the one who met his end
She was searching for her lost long-time friend

She wondered where her mate had gone
But she had a sixth sense nervous inkling
Seeing the butcher was too friendly and all
When he kept kind of nervously winking

That all was not what it should be
Balanced on her mind as a weight
She figured she should turn back off
Something in his eyes made her hesitate

Her hunger would have to wait
Then the butcher turned his back
When she heard the telephone ring
She started to feel all a-quiver
Was she being sold down the river?
Was she another order on another sting?

She looked askance at his stance
His hands seemed to talk about her
He moved as if waiting for a chance
In that instance she glimpsed her future

Could she trust the butcher in leafy Bristol
Seeing what his wielding cleaver could bring
Knowing her life would not be improved
She ran as fast as her legs could move
She could see her future as clear as crystal
She decided to go when he grabbed a pistol
Though she could not read she saw the writing
The symbols said to her staying was not inviting
They reminded her of the squiggles on the I-Ching
Fear ran right through her making her heart ring
The feeling touched the instinct of her mainspring
Seeing his sign showed he was trained in Beijing

A Dog is just for the Pandemic

A Dog is just for the Pandemic
He lied to those at the sanctuary
Then he needed some company
Now the day came to cast aside the stray
Tied to a lamppost then casually walked away

A Dog is just for the Pandemic
It's so cute on the sparky Instagram
You can meet and greet in a flim-flam
Then when he had to go back to work
Sent her to a sanctuary as a knee-jerk scam

A Dog is just for the Pandemic
When you feel lonely and have no job
A dog does not care if you are a slob
But when he worked out what she had cost
Took her to the Motorway where she was lost

A Dog is just for the Pandemic
You can take him for a walk everyday
They will be loyal and listen to what you say
But the beauty is when their race has been ran
You can just get rid of it just because you can

A Dog is just for the Pandemic
They are great for playing in the park
And you feel safe with them in the dark
But when they scratch the furniture and trunk
You have to sling them out as so much junk

A Dog is just for the Pandemic
It is nonsense to say you have it for life
After all it is just a pooch not a wife
And when you have a new baby and all
A mutt is a burden if she's learning to crawl

The question is no longer academic
An animal is just part of the epidemic
It is not worth any moral polemic
After the success of the vivisection vaccination
Put the pooch in a pool on a permanent vacation

A Dog is just for the Pandemic
The solution is plain and systemic
Forget any sentiment if it is 'dangerous'
They are already far too numerous
And when you are out on a Sunday jolly
Let it off a leash and spend your lolly
If it happens to bite someone
At least you can get rid of her
In some grumpy judge's court
Where she will get a legal penance
When the thing will be sentenced

It is only the death of a pet for your folly
Who cares as next time you can be choosy
You could even click and collect a collie

Shylock's Blood

What is so special about black people anyway?
Was what the politician asked
But he did not remain long enough to find an answer
What is so special about black people anyway?
Was the question that fell from his lips
But he always thought too much thought was a cancer

What is so special about women?
The priest asked as if he was still in confession
Though he was far from the box of silence
What is so special about women?
He used communion to abuse every choirboy
As a daily distraction from his own violence

What is so special about speciesism?
Asked all the anti-social protesters
As they marched and waved placards and swore
What is so special about speciesism?
When the confederate flags were unfurled
As they asked for a T-bone and demanded more

Then out of the crowd
A voice cried out loud
As a fishmonger bull without a bullhorn
He stood tall and proud
Not caring if it was allowed
And then declared 'I wish I was never born'

You have treated me as if I did not matter
Injecting malice in blunder land
As if I had no value and I am one to batter
My eyes hurt too and my heart bleeds blue
And my mind and pulse and soul
Beats fast with a blood that pours
The bleeding cuts me to the core
The rain of pain makes me roar
Yet Shylock my heart is the same as yours

The Missionary and the Cannibal

Dave explained 'I eat fish and chicken'
And told us 'it's middle-class hypocrisy'
Making the finger-lickin' action
A perfect reason with no moral distraction

Dave is hardly a hypocrite
As it is only a little bit
Much like the Founding Fathers
Who declared as their prequel
'A self-evident truth all men are created equal'
Then proved it was a lie as there was no sequel

They meant all white American men
Who did not include anyone defined
As black or Indian or otherwise
So judges closed their prejudicial eyes
A fact that found support in the courts
Who declared with such an ease
Like a roe deer running wild
Were people they classed as Chinese

As for women well they should stay in the kitchen
Where they keep busy plucking a chicken
Or the bedroom where they can perhaps be picked
By a Wienstein-type with the feeling of criminals
For all women that the law has for all animals

The lesson Dave wants us to learn
Borne of his own values
As he is no kind of squit
Means he too must earn
And not seek to hide behind
A self-imposed label of hypocrite
It is a pale excuse as he taps his nose
That cannot stand scrutiny as he knows
Trying to pass it off only shows
A weak-kneed 'I know I shouldn't but...'

It is no different however it is put
Rest assured it is the same for sure
As someone saying 'I love animals,
But I like eating them more'

Any which way you look at it
It comes back to the same track
Dave acts in the way he does
Because he can
Because he is a man
Because an animal is a brand
It is grand to eat their flesh
And it salivates with the mesh
That drools from his lips and gathers
On his hips so the oil on his fingertips
Is not just gravy
But mixed in the bud with their blood

Dress up reason as a half-hearted excuse
So they remain under our thumbscrew
Because the belief of people like Dave
Makes the killing a choice
Not between two evils
But no evil at all:
For to kill someone alive is the choice
Made easier because that someone
Is a legal thing with no legal voice

In being a hypocrite
Rather than a hero or mentor we can see
Attenborough is perhaps like you and me
Much as the cannibals saw the missionaries
And almost started to believe
The sermons the Christians delivered
They eagerly were willing to receive
Yet when their belief was tested
They believed food was too good to waste
So the missionaries were boiled alive
Human lobsters with an even better taste

The problem is when you are hailed
As the most trusted man on the planet
You cannot afford to be seen
As one who acts as one more gannet
The danger is instead of one to inspire
You can be one whose tongue is on fire
Everything takes second-place to our desire
By those who parade lies as a password
Will steal your ideas as a thief of fire
Then use them as the currency of a liar
So animals die while they quietly conspire

From BLM to ALM Stem-by-Stem

Jonno the bozo talks with a twisted tongue
Speaks racist sleaze in a sentence strung
With weasel words filed with sour wiles
He then brands children out of hand
Dumped and out-trumped as another bunch of
'Piccaninnies with watermelon smiles'

When slave trader Colston's statue crumbled
His warped heart and tarnished soul tumbled
Into the murky graveyard of the dark dock water
His rancid fame spelled in linked chains
With a face as infested as his remains
Of sad-eyed slaves he stole
And sold and slaughtered

Colston and Jonno embraced fixed false faces
Serves just to remind us of slave traces
So we shout about and call out to condemn
From Uncle Tom to Jim Crow's Klan pride
While slaves and dogs were hung side-by-side
Springing from BLM to ALM stem-by-stem

Raise a fist to forget Patel and bend a strong knee
For a misplaced race demanding their place in history
Close the link between BLM and ALM
Make your mark with a single stinging stem
Now is the time and this is the place
To recognise lies etched in each frozen face
Of traders selling animals and black men
Whether wild or a child none were immune
As chains clanked beneath a white-hot moon
Lives held by a string from heart to hem
Balanced by worth in diamonds and a gem
Springing from BLM to ALM stem-by-stem

Freedom's flower blooms with every stem
From BLM to the same stem for ALM
It is time to rise and make some gentle mayhem
As a burning requiem for the torch of ALM

Wipe the sweat from your brow
We are all Stag-spanners now
Resist phoney Latin to amuse his jaundiced kin
And the lies sold in a greed-drive reef
Chlorinated chickens and cancer-drugged beef
Selling animals down the river in a slave skin

149

Raise a fist to forget Patel and bend a strong knee
For a righteous place in revolution and world history
Close the link between BLM and ALM
Make your mark with a single stinging stem
To sin by silence when we should protest
Makes cowards out of the best and all women

The Horsemen of Hate

Why is it so hard for you to see
That the sum of the misery
Adds up to the acts
Of those whose repose
Is only a change of clothes
The Naked Emperor wore
In the guise of Custer's bribery
While you wallow in the luxury
You find in a closed soul
Combined with a perfect blind mind?

A horseman of the apocalypse
Whose message is lost on your lips
Until it is far too late
For will we ever realise

Even as our bullets make the sky cry
We will still close our eyes
Using lies as our angling bait
As the five horsemen of hate

Salt 'saw deep in the eyes of the animals
The human soul look out' upon him
Borne of a wisdom he has seen and known
Yet we rest on every whim
Of any fanciful notion
Making every one our victim
While we fail to vault
Our fault in the vision of Salt
We know the eyes of a horse
Reflects his image and our own
A truth we have tried to divorce

The Animals War of Independence

No kindred soul in chained Jim Crow
No Mississippi Chinese Compliment
No whip on his much-marked back
No whip on the horse on the track
No hanging on the Strange Fruit tree
No gallows for the stray dog born free

Forget your tired lies to fire us
With half-baked ideas on a virus
So the vaquita slowly dies
To satisfy your trumpet lies
Ringing on a cure by medicine
Between your crime and cardinal sin

Between the lines of Manchu Wuhu
Drying your wet markets is overdue
Even you know your claims are untrue
Damn your wet markets damn you
With your blood-curled flag unfurled
Locking poached pets in your underworld

Save your lies for someone
Who will listen and even believe
Anyone who is easily deceived
While you christen lies as forsooth
Our tongue touches your gnawing tooth

No religious ritual slaughter
No barbed hooks in the water
No wet market Pinnochio
No more buffalo Custer blow
No kindred soul in chains
No dog-whistle Jim Crow

Coulrophobia Blues

When I told the other birds
I was going to be a singer
How they all laughed at me
When I said I had a voice
That would make a bird jealous
Just you wait and see
The laughter grew louder
As I grew silent with lockjaw
They yelled 'we are seeking a sound'
So just tell us

When I told the grazing cows
I was going to be a poet
How they all laughed at me
When I said I had a way with a word

That had to be heard
Just you wait and see
The laughter grew louder
As I shrank on the blank page
No bells chimed as I had no sense
Of rhythm or rhyme

When I told them all
I was going to be a class clown
Then you too laughed at me
When I said my sadness
Was deeper than Garibaldi rust
Just you wait and see
I was boiled alive to satisfy
Your hungry biased eyes
Your laughter scalded me
As I burned in the Grimaldi dust

I was fooling while my unsprung tongue was silent
I remained being seen as a forever vacant savant
I told you I had no desire to die
Before I was even born
If I could I would bet you are not laughing now
For when you read this it will be
Only my lonely abattoir epitaph
Is all that you will know and see
So at last please let me be to R I P

Who sees the real You

Confucius said we should not do anything
To others that we would not do to ourselves
Though whether he said that after seeing
The bodies on the abattoir shelves
The bodies on the butchers' shelves
The bodies on the circus shelves
The bodies on the designer shelves
The bodies on the experimenters' shelves
The bodies on the freedom-fighters' shelves
The bodies on the gallow-birds' shelves
The bodies on the hook shop shelves
Without a fair-minded honest jury of twelve
That can analyse lies and continue to delve
Remains as unknown as his shrunken bones
Yet we know that unlike Pilate and Judas
The lesson worth the learning
Was the one lived by the noble Confucius

The Virus of love Revisited

Down so low I could not see what was up
You held my splintered soul in your heart's cup
Reached my waving hand with a wounded paw
Leading me on the ladder of love's law

There were times that I was not strong enough
When I buckled as the road was too rough
You rescued me with tough words straight and true
Now if I roam all roads lead back to you

I feel as free as wild bees in the trees
Pleased to be caught by your love-bird disease
Freed by the fever of your luck-filled love
Locked and lost in the virus of your love

I fought the lonely 3 a.m. feeling
Fixed on the only one my heart thought of
My mind was mixed up and rocked and reeling
Calmed by your touch as tender as a velvet glove
Though through that long night
I was filled with lonely fright
My lonesome spirit was askew and still raging
My mind was rambling and my body was aging
You proved the one contagion worth catching
Is the flame-filled virus of love

You may not know the language
You may not know the words
You may not know my name
Yet as a lifeline giver what you delivered
As the last arrow in your love's quiver
Saved me and is strictly not for the birds

Skewer the Skies

Emmett Till was stilled and brought down
By a pack of cloaked cult clowns
Hiding behind their hoods of hate
He could not escape from their fate
Towards the nature of his birth
For them he had no value or worth
He was placed in a race he could never win
Emmett Till was killed at will due to his skin

Rem'mie Fells had a tale that tells
How prejudice in action smells
When the cop with the burning gun
Aimed and shot to kill 'another one'
With no way to retreat or retrack
Rem'mie was felled pell-mell
Because she was a woman born black

A cold blooded cop was hot on the trail
Of a man whose life was up for sale
At a knock down price below the pale
Too much trouble to take him to gaol
Chauvin held him tight in the gutter
Kneeing his windpipe to stop his mutter
For more than 500 seconds
While his lifeblood drains as death beckons
Who cares about his shouts
'Please, I can't breathe'
Then he cried, 'Help me Mama'
While his life was unsheathed
Chauvin pressed even harder
Through teeth that seethed
As if holding a trapped animal
One who made the cops annoyed
His plea for mercy served
As an epitaph for George Floyd
He was part of America's bric-a-brac
Meeting three cops hunting in a pack
Given his crime he had no way back
A death sentence for being born black

Sadder than all the pleas for mercy
Was his desperate final plea
For his Mama could not save him
She had had her own date with destiny

The slaves forced to pick cotton
And the gains all ill-gotten
Should never be forgotten
For us they were animals in kind
We abused and sent to their graves
Though the change in 1865
Supposed to protected those still alive
Failed to protect our animal slaves
Then as now they never forgave
Losing a War as abuse was their reference
Whether the victim is an animal or a slave
For them there remains no difference

Let's poison all the trees and bees
Let's count the profit we will seize
Let's keep spraying a toxic pesticide
Let's destroy all of the countryside
Let's forget the squashed hedgehogs
Let's forget all the underdogs
Let's keep turning the biased cogs
Who cares and who counts the cost
Animals in bloody mud in our Holocaust

Save your idle words for the tumbrel to fill
Until you realise the ghost of Martha White is right
She still proves truth is more than black and white
Until you're ready to skewer the skies with sparks
Showering the world with the spirit of Rosa Parks

Don't wait for a death-bed confession
Like De La Beckwith the killer in 1955
Save for him Emmett would still be alive
So don't call me at all
Until you march in Medger Evers memory
Until you listen to George Floyd's final plea
Until you hear the shrill of each animal we kill
Until you're ready to save the next Emmett Till

One Man's Grouse/One Man's Gross

One man thinks it is grand to shoot grouse
Yet one says such action makes him a louse
He says you do not understand the countryside
He goes so far as to say they are all one-eyed
Though whether he means the birds or sabs
Is not clear as one-eyed
Might be the grouse who died
It could be the jack and queens
What he means is the dead-eyed
Face of the blue-bird
As the hunters in a herd
Blast them from the skies
While the one-eyed jacks stare away from justice
In a way that equally must see the pus that this
Wounded bird exudes as the hunters drink
To the health of those that they bagged
As their blood ran hot and truth was gagged
Sharing thoughts of how many they killed
Being so thrilled by the blood they spilled
While the second man might even be right
Given that the one-eyed could be
The staring face of Janus
Known to be false-eyed
As having been phoney tinker
Talking from his straining sphincter
Yet it could be one man is on song
For even one who is always wrong

Can by chance be right
Regardless of the peril
So the one with a mind defiled
Would try to justify rape of the wild
Sometimes much as a biased man
Is forced to see a harsh truth
For even a purblind hunter
Used to babble purely feral
Could stumble over a squirrel

Goodbye Doctor Li

The WHO knew the Chinese
As eager as ever to please
Their case sprang from Xmas 2019
That was what made them keen

Before he could inspire us
Before he was sent to prison
Before he got the virus
Before he died for his vision

Doctor Li Wenliang was blessed with proof
The Chinese compliment was a total spoof
A virus spread from animal to a human
And then with each animal shoo-in
From a hot corpse with a tight throat
Animal to human to animal in Wuhan

Nothing could be denied
Though the Chinese tried
That their money is our market's wraith
So the price of fried rice is cut and dried

They heard the whistle-blower
Deliver a message that banged
Against the walls of the hospital
Too late to fill his repeated pang
When the virus that laid him low
Led to the death of Dr Li Wenliang

Blues for Charlie Hebdo

The teacher committed the final crime
He dared to ridicule a religion
Not just any old stool pigeon
As in pornography or Christianity
Or some odd Seventh Day Adventist
The type of eternal optimist

The teacher committed the sacred crime
As the bells of Rhymney chime
With a doom-laden sound
As Samuel Paty is remembered
For being dismembered by some zealot
Thinking they have a monopoly on truth
When they can issue a crass fatwa
Who can hound a man to death
Who can stone a woman to death
Who can claim it is such a religion
And then kill animals in a cruel ruse
The barbaric ritual slaughter
That is simply animal abuse
Dressed up as a religious excuse

Think of the profit in ritually killing an animal
Forget the victim as it is much more subliminal
Search for a false ritual to find the real criminal

As they want to please their palate
And it is only a bleeding animal
When it bellows as it bleeds to death
Upside down on the abattoir floor
A notch below a woman
A pace behind a camel
Their lives are untrammelled
As killing is their business
In the name of religion
So another day writ in water
With the mathematics multiplying
The profits gained by ritual slaughter
They figure they have a monopoly on truth
Yet you do not have to be any kind of sleuth
Seeing them hide behind a robe and mask
Without being asked and gives a sign
Saying you remind me of the blind lawyer
Searching for a defence dressed as a reason
While trying to avoid a true charge of treason

Finally the prophet asked about Pilate
Who posed the question 'What is truth?'
Then had the grace to save face by walking away
Unlike you whose values follow the false muse
To use abuse as a religious ruse
Then drink the water of oblivion
The prophet declared kindness to all beings

With eyes seeing no need for the greed
Of the voyeur and the Greek poseur
Showing less bottle than biased Aristotle
As everyone who follows a religion
That devalues animals as their property
Intent on using their quirky zeal
To throttle free speech and liberty

All religions advocate kindness to animals
To practice abuse is just a religious excuse
Whatever rite and ruse they may try to use
Reason is not delivered by a bludgeon
Anymore than violence as their oxygen
It is time to sing Charlie Hebdo's Blues
As an unchained charter we can use
To fight for the right to be free from abuse
Whether she is a pangolin or a pachyderm
She is born to live on her own terms
Charlie Hebdo explored the vestibule
Of ideas as a straight moral rule
No religion is immune from ridicule
Whether delivered by a genius or a fool
Charlie Hebdo delivered a spool
Of truth in their cartoon panorama
Like the great and good in Tell Mama
Terrorists' lies shattered by Faith Matters
The silence of treason dealt a blow
Their vigilance clearing the cesspool
By the sign of Westergaard and Hebdo
Using truth as their tale-telling tool

Straight from the Trainer's Fingers

Gordon Elliott is so photogenic
A model trainer on Morgan
It is a pity it is tragic
That he has no vital organ

Gordon Elliott puts up two fingers
And grinning as he makes a call
The frozen photo still lingers
The fat trainer astride his last fall

Gordon Elliott smiles from ear to ear
Captures a smile for the camera
The horse is the last thing on his mind
Between the shutter and slaughterman

Morgan earned cash for the man
He died on his gallops in 2019
Now one more dead horse can be seen
On the stilled Twitter screen RIP

Elliott will train another horse
Who will run and run of course
And if he loses his life at the source
Remember no one gives a monkey's
For like Morgan he is just a horse

Elliot sits with all his weight
Sprawled across the dead horse
Showing contempt rather than remorse
For being caught by the camera's glare
Perhaps it would not matter
If it was just a donkey
Then Elliot's fate would less
As it would be one more flunkey

Songbird

I used to hear the songbird
Singing in the morning
I used to hear her singing
Chirping without warning
I used to hear her song
Every day and all day long
It made me sing inside
Along with her fluting song

I miss her and think about her fate
Wonder why in the unfathomable way
That life works there was no reason
For her to lose to a vanity-stricken
Ego-driven narcissistic trophy hunter
Using her bullets as bait
With nothing to offer
But her contaminated hate

With any luck the next duck
She shoots from the sky
Will by chance land on her
And by surprise take her off-guard

As her ever-itchy finger
Still on the trigger
She pulls as he falls
Given fate can be fickle
So the hail of bullets
As she was forced to pull it
Is released on her genitals
All in all blows away her brains
At the same time as her balls

The hero and the fork-tongued Farmer

Leon Yeneews was a farmer who had a long and healthy respect for all the animals who had given him a good living all his life. Or at least that was his constant claim. He was so attached to them that on the odd occasion he even gave them names. That was handy when it came to the roll call in sorting out the next candidate for the one-way ticket to the slaughterhouse. Sometimes the animals had particular attributes that made Yeneews pleased or even proud of their prowess. He was especially taken with one of the unnamed animals because of the speed at which he raced around the field. He galloped across the grass yet he only had three legs. The front right one was missing. He was a favourite of Yeneews because he liked all pigs above other animals, but this one had wound itself into Yeneews affection because he so strove to overcome his apparent disability. Sometimes he just stood there looking over the 5-bar gate and stared admiringly at the three-legged pig. Sometimes he just gave the three-legged pig more food than the others or even fed him separately so his was the only snout in the trough.

Sometimes the fancy just took him and he allowed the three-legged pig to ramble into the kitchen where he would stroke him and tickle his soft head. The pig would stand still and look up at Yeneews as if he was enjoying the feeling of being treated like a family pet. On one memorable occasion a travelling salesman straight out of every pub anecdote happened to be passing by when he, Deke Rivers, was so taken with the three-legged pig that he pulled up, got out of his car and much like the farmer, stared at him. The farmer greeted Rivers and the two of them stared in mutual appreciation at the antics of the three-legged pig. As if he was performing for them, he raced and over-balanced and stumbled and fell over, yet in an instant rolled over and got up. Then he did the same thing over and over again. It was as if the fact he was missing a leg was a 'party trick' because he could barely run fast for long without falling over in a heap.

Nevertheless, every time he fell, straightway he got up again and then raced until he fell again. All in all the spectacle caused the farmer and the salesman to both gaze in silent admiration and laugh hysterically in unison when he kept falling over. After a short while the salesman moved a bit closer to the farmer and engaged him in conversation. Following a few pleasantries the conversation continued in a somewhat strange surprising way:

Deke Rivers: What a truly wonderful picture he is, look at him.

Leon Yeneews: You're right there, son.

DR: He looks so happy. Is he always like that?

LY: He's as happy as pig in shite all day and all night, tell you the truth. It's just the way he is, the way he's always been.

DR: I'll bet you're proud of him aren't you?

LY: You're right there, son, rightly proud.

DR: He seems to be managing so well with his loss of a limb, if you don't mind me saying so.

LY: No. No, I don't mind at all. After all he's special, really special.

DR: In what way? What. Over the fact he's coping with just three-legs?

LY: Oh yeah. That pig's an 'ero. I tell you.

DR: What do you mean?

LY: I tell you, he's an 'ero.

DR: Yes, I understand that, but what do you actually mean when you say 'he's a hero'?

LY: Well, everything he's done like son. Tell you the truth he saved my life.

DR: Are you serious? He saved your life?

LY: Yeah, and more than once, son, believe me.

DR: What saved your bacon?

LY: I know you won't believe it, but that's the first time I've heard that comment – today that is.

DR: Right, but what did he do? How did he save your life?

LY: Well I was driving me tractor when I suddenly felt unwell. My chest banged like a drum and I had a heart attack. I collapsed. The tractor was out of control and was heading straight for the farmhouse. If it hit the house, the speed it was going, it would have demolished the wall and might have killed the wife. Even worse, that would've damaged my tractor.

DR: So what did the pig do?

LY: I didn't know at the time, son, 'cos I was collapsed. But he jumped onto the tractor, changed the gear and pulled the brake on so it came to a juddering, shuddering halt.

DR: Wow!

LY: That pig, I tell you, he's an 'ero. He saved my wife, saved my life. He even watched by me until the ambulance came to take me to the hospital. He's an 'ero.

DR: I can barely believe it. A pig saving lives. It's remarkable.

LY: Oh, that's not all he's done.

DR: Really, he's done more?

LY: He saved my life twice, son.

DR: Tell me more. What did he do?

LY: Well, I was in the kitchen one day and I turned to go indoors to get my pipe. I turned too sharply and lost my balance. In order to steady myself I grabbed the handle of the chip pan. The whole thing exploded. The kitchen was on fire. I couldn't find my way back to get out.

DR: So what happened? How did you escape?

LY: I didn't.

DR: What do you mean, you didn't?

LY: That pig, I tell he's an 'ero. He rescued me. He hammered head on through the flames. I was on the floor. I couldn't breathe. Out cold. Well, not exactly cold. He caught me sleeve in his snout and dragged me out.

DR: Crikey. That's truly incredible. Obviously I don't doubt your word, but I can hardly believe it. No wonder you describe the pig as a hero.

LY: Ah, that's not all.

DR: Surely there's no more to the story? What else could the creature do? He's rescued you twice when all is said and done.

LY: Yeah, but he even saved his brethren.

DR: His brethren? What is he, a part-time vicar?

LY: No, I mean the other animals, his brothers and sisters on the farm. We love the animals so much you see that's how we see them, describe them, even think of them. Really as part of the family, all of 'em.

DR: I see. So what else did he do?

LY: It's like this. I know some farmers don't mind the hunt on their land. I'm not one of them. I've always hated it because it's so goddam cruel, setting 40 hounds on a single fox to tear it to pieces. Believe me if you ever heard a fox scream in agony as they rip the animal apart, you'd be against it too. Farmer or no farmer, it don't matter. I hate those cowards, everything about them.

DR: Yes, I understand, but what did the pig do? How did he save the other animals from the hunters and their hounds?

LY: Well, I'll be brief because I've got to round the herd up. Besides, it's quite a long-drawn out story. Anyway the hunters and the hounds, a whole marauding mob of them, came onto my land and terrorised the cows. They were all in calf too. Think how much they're worth. Think how much I'd stand to lose. They were all surrounded by the horses and the hounds. They were terrified. They ran way as fast as they could as if their fat arses were on fire.

DR: So how did the pig help you?

LY: He saw the lead huntsman and he got on top of the bales of straw and as he was riding by he jumped on him, knocked him clean off his horse and then proceeded to kick the living daylights out of him. All the horses and, for that matter, all the others were spooked by the jumping pig so they bolted out of my field and the huntsman, frightened for his life, ran as fast as he could, as fast as his legs would take him off of my land.

I tell you this for nothing. I've never had any trouble since from the hunt again. They won't be in a hurry again to return. Not with my 'ero around.

DR: Well, I don't know what else to say. Frankly I'm simply astonished that you have got such a splendid creature. He's one in a million, if not more. No wonder you say he's a hero. How else could you describe him?

LY: That's true enough, son. I could never part with him.

DR: So he's not destined for the abattoir?

LY: Oh no, I couldn't bear to do that to him.

DR: As you have been so open in telling me about the pig's exploits, I hope you won't mind if I ask you something about him?

LY: No, not at all. You go ahead, son. Ask me anything you like about my favourite pig.

DR: I wondered, how did he lose his leg?

LY: Well that's obvious ain't it?

DR: You mean he was born that way?

LY: No

DR: He was trapped by the tractor when he rescued you?

LY: No.

DR: He was burned by the fire when he rescued you?

LY: No.

DR: The huntsman attacked him or this horse kicked him so hard he went lame? It had to be amputated?

LY: No.

DR: If it was none of those things, how did he lose his leg?

LY: We ate it.

DR: To be honest I'm slightly taken aback. Isn't that awfully cruel after all he's done for you? To leave him in that condition when he's saved your life twice. Isn't that truly cruel?

LY: No, that's what he's bred for. Don't forget I saved him from the slaughterhouse. So he's got to be thankful to me for saving his life. As well as feeding him all this time.

DR: I see. That's one way of looking at it I suppose, but why didn't you put the poor creature out of his misery and just kill him? Then you could've eaten the complete pig? Wouldn't that be better?

LY: Oh no, I wouldn't dream of doing that. I couldn't do that and sleep at night. I'd have an uneasy conscience. That's the last thing I'd do even if I was desperate. No, not me. Don't forget he's part of our family.

DR: Why?

LY: Why? You ask me why?

DR: Yes, why?

LY: Because the pig's an 'ero.

DR: What difference does that make to you?

LY: You couldn't eat a pig like that all at once.

The Phantom Vivisector

They strapped her in the cage
Bound her to the cold steel bars
Committed every scientific outrage
That they could gauge as both engaged
Injecting her arms and legs and chest
Into her head and brain and the rest
Then they injected poison in her eyes
When they were both bloodshot
They removed them in the time-slot

So they focused on the clock
By taking all her body apart
Leaving nothing intact except her heart
As they noted the data statistics
Part curiosity and wholly egotistic
When they finished stripping her bones
So she was just a blind skeleton
Their repeated experiment ended
When they swiftly killed their exhibit

The sabs broke into the secret lab
Balaclava clad in black vigilantes
And kidnapped the vivisectionist
To let him visit the circle of Dante

They prodded and probed his body
Then tracked the terrain of his insides
To trace what was there besides
The skill he had as a vivisector
As science's natural benefactor

They searched his body again
Up and down and down and up
With no regard to his pain
Though their search was in vain
To make sure they did everything
They even searched for his soul
Nevertheless they could never guess
The one organ they could not kick-start
They tried and failed to find his heart

They were flummoxed because it was
A conclusion they found hard to resist
Despite the instruments and scalpel minds
The sabs came to a confused conclusion
That proved to be a twist upon a twist
They failed to add his heart to their list
Though there was no reason to panic
For the absence was purely organic
Far from being an existential quest
They were defeated by truth's tempest
It was not something they had missed
What the sabs were seeking did not exist

In Alpaca land the executioner is the King

There is a cloudy nirvana
Some distance across the stream
Where if you really listen
You can hear a seal silently scream

There is a clear nirvana
Whose secret is in the silver ring
That has a sight for wide eyes
Seeing the executioner is the King

There is a dark nirvana
Where truth has no store
As each one lines up
So the score is more and more

There is a faded nirvana
That has no meaning now
For every one that is alive
There is another dead cow

After the laughter
And the shifting sands
There is the sound
Of the pound as it clinks

Across a hidden heart
That was a mouth
Before their nerve ends
Were randomly cut
Then it went south
And now it is in
Someone else's mouth

Marooned rats leave the Ship

In the 18th century
There was shipwreck
In the Indian Ocean
Almost Christmas near Christmas Island
Where the sailors met a watery grave
And the black rats had another notion
So they swam to the island
In search of food and a home
And soon found both after risking
The briny foam
The killed the chicks for kicks
And pillaged the eggs of the seabirds
So the birds became food for the rats
And the birds were an endangered species
Where the cycle of life and death
Especially the reefs
Were in danger from the rats
Who were no less than
And almost as bad as human thieves
So now we can drop poison
From the sky
To catch the rats
And bleed them dry
As it is a drone
That is cheap and quick
And after all only kills
A pack of rats

While making sure
The chicks and eggs are preserved
So they can be served up as a pirate's breakfast
And as for any more shipwrecked sailors
Though perhaps like the eternal jailer
The rats on board will head
Full steam ahead for their bread
Back onto the infested Island again
While the rat pack politicos
Boast about their notion
Of killing two birds with one stone
By never leaving the wildlife alone
With their mission in motion
First is how to make the sky die
Second is to destroy the ocean

A Shark in shallow Waters

Into the shallow water
The huge troubled fish sailed on
His fin was broken
His body was shot
His race was run
He floated in shock
His blow-hole was blocked

All the people gathered around
When they heard the pained sound
Of the foreign creature they found
Bobbing through the surface sea
As he struggled on the quicksand
They moved closer as a band
Intending to lend a helping hand

He had been injured and knocked
He was bleeding and land-locked

Although he was distressed and all alone
The people figured with their help
He would soon be on his way home

People multiplied to make sure he did not die
Vets and cast nets and the cranes and the planes
All gathered to rescue the massive bleeding fish
From the trapped dish of sinking sand
As his life was being swiftly extinguished

When finally after sweat and toil
Of days and days on end
Their effort came to the boil
People on the quayside and pier
Shouted and clapped and cheered
When the giant was set free
To sail on home into the inviting sea

Ropes were removed so he could sway
With the sparkling ship as his guide
Lest he became prey to a nomad shark
As the sea left him nowhere to hide
The wide-eyed ship sailed alongside
As the wary Star Chamber sailors
Helped him towards his home
Yet he looked weary and so alone

Out of sight of the shore
The sailors spoke to each other
Then gave a knowing nod
That was readily understood

Though there was no pod
One would be enough for today
It would satisfy the glinted eye
Of the search and research
All in the name of science
They loaded a fancy appliance

Out of sight of those waving from the shore
Time was running out and they had to score

His bleeding pleading eyes met theirs
They were busy with their own affairs
His silent plea seemed lost in the surging sea

As the appliance was unsheathed
The huge fish no longer breathed
As the ship that had rescued him
Unveiled the Star Chamber flag
Then all too soon
Beneath the freezing moon
They took the giant's life
By their honed harpoon
Through the swirling sea they fled
Leaving the ocean clothed in red
With blood and blubber and body
Spread on the ship's bed
His colour matched their masthead

Research was a tag they used with ease
Covering every kind of known disease
Research was a word they used for lies
Keeping truth hidden from prying eyes
As if research was an infectious disease
Though in the main a variety of greed
The sailors and crew did as they pleased
Not caring one iota about foreign legalese
For the harpoon-laden ship was Japanese

Cycle of Life

She said with the voice of experience
That the children look after each animal
And finally kill them and eat them
That is the lesson they have learned about life
And how to manage their natural strife
Sometimes the answer is a kitchen knife
She said it was a vital lesson to learn
For in simple terms it is the cycle of life

While as any mother she meant well
It was strange she failed to tell
That what she was teaching them
Was opposite the words that fell
From her tongue to those so young
For the dead were always the dead
Because they were hamstrung
By the lack of a human tongue

Each creature they cared for
Could be killed and eaten
As their lives were fleeting
And their deaths the cost
They were bound to pay
Because in the cycle of life
Their palate guides the decision
It is as it is as it is the only way

To all her children
With no pause for breath
She was selling her ideal
Ignore what the animal feels
That was a natural prelude
As a reward for feeding them
Animals were their recycled food

Then the youngest child asked
Mum you say it's good to treat our pet
As if it was splitting a hunk of wood
No reason to fret
Or for any regret
Yet that seems less like life we respect
And more like our own cycle of death

Voyage of *The Zong*

In 1781 Captain Luke Collingwood
Claimed he had no choice
He had to rely on his inner voice
His cargo was in danger
He had to protect the property
As the content was somewhat stranger
So they tried hard to hide
By using a kind of embargo
By chance Olandah Equino discovered
The content of the overloaded cargo

Claiming they were running out of water
His choice was between making a profit
And losing the money he would forfeit
He had to decide who counted for squit

The ship was laden with so many slaves
There was no easy answer as to who to save
Because the decision counted for more than
Some children and women and many black men

One-by-one the sailors threw the slaves
Into the deep merciless stormy waves
Day-after-day for three full days
Collingwood ordered the sailors
To throw the men women and children
To their chained water-filled graves
Until 133 slaves sank beneath the waves

The case of the slaves was sheer despair
As the chains dragged them down
Far below the unforgiving sea
Their deaths as certain as a slaves' misery
Their cries drowned as they were too
At the bottom of the ocean red and blue

The case involved more than bees and honey
It revolved around a claim for insurance money
So the decision had to be one that would convince
A tough Judge whose knowledge was never runny

Lord Mansfield weighed each term of the contract
He balanced what mattered in loss and gain
His judgment was nothing to do with the impact
He was not judging the deaths or even pain
His only concern was to follow the money train

Then what *The Zong Case* finally decided
When Mansfield followed the legal course
Of judging the farrago of the unwanted cargo
The value of a slave was half that of a horse

Granville Sharp tried in vain
To name and try the murderous crew
But as it was only a cash-valued cargo
The law defeated what he sought to do
Collingwood escaped his earthly justice
Though he had an almighty price to pay
Like the 133 slaves he murdered
Fate captured the seafarer torturer
For before he could be tried
He joined that cargo no-return journey
While on terra firma he collapsed and died
Finally facing his own judgement day

Tulsa Massacre Anniversary 1921-2021

In June 1921 the rednecks led the mob
Against the blameless black community
Based and built on a blatant lie
They saw their opportunity
To use Jim Crow law
To demolish the buildings and churches
And homes and murder 300 black people
On their bent principles and crooked steeple
In a veiled genocide

Yet the rednecks of Tulsa
Wore their badge of dishonour
With a perverted pride
Having razed the hospital to the ground
They sought to raze their hate from history
By making their massacre a mystery

Nevertheless truth can never be hidden
Whatever the De La Beckwiths of the world
Figure when their life flag is unfurled

In two days they murdered 300 people
10,000 men and women and children
Were rendered homeless by their unity
Of redneck prejudice and purpose
To destroy the complete community
By arson and looting and lynching
They tried to hang Dick Rowland
For no reason save being black
And everyone on the wrong side
Of the redneck racist Tulsa track

Burgling the home of an 80-year-old man
Paralyzed and too crippled to walk
His wife begged for his life
A witness says 'the damn dogs shot him'
Then they torched his home
For good measure they murdered his wife

Then they found a black blind man
With no legs who moved on wheels
The mob roped him like a steer
Tied him to the back of a truck
And laughed as they pulled him
Up and down Main Street
As he squealed like a stuck pig

They revved with even greater zeal
Firing the night with an executioner's seal
He died beneath their spinning wheels

Then they found Andrew Cheesten Jackson
The surgeon held his hands up in surrender
Instead the committed cold-blooded murder
Cut down by two trigger-happy white offenders
Though he pleaded for his life
Their bullets took their toll
Bleeding to death before their eyes
While they saw his murder as their prize
He could not be saved in the only hospital
That served the black people all around
Caught in their hate-filled bubble
The hospital was just a pile of rubble
The mob had burned it to the ground

Yet who were the rednecks
And who was not is easy to check
Like the German citizens and the Nazi's
The Tulsa cops and the owners of shops
The businessmen and the mayor
Were all part of the play and players
Even the judge could not be fussed to budge
Instead they wiped the memory of the dead
From the history of their story and warped glory

Because they knew that every man
Who murdered the 300 guiltless black people
Were or sided with the guilt-riddled Klan

A hundred years later
Though the Tulsa authorities
Tried to bury the truth
Not realising no one can escape
From its natural superiority

A group of mourners gathered around
Some felt a magnetic pull
They dug where they stood
And found mass graves of those
Who were buried in the clothes
They died in when the murderous
Tulsa redneck citizens were barbarous
Their deeds were discovered
As truth always is regardless of the clutches
For despite their desperate attempts to hide
Their deeds could never be concealed
When their attempt at ethnic genocide
Of people holding the bones of their pets
Spoke with the earthquake of death
The victims' magnetic voice revealed
Nothing could hide the multiple-murder
That all the skeletons concealed

What was doomed to fail as every dog knows
When he buries a bone however far from home
The grave never forgets however deep the ruth
The taste on his wisdom tooth
Will never be strong enough to bury truth

White is right about being Black

Martha was always the one
Who knew from the start
That she had to ignite
The fire inside her heart
When she was dog-tired
And tired of being treated like a dog
Not allowed to sit down on a bus
And addressed as if she was a hog
She knew it was time for action
Against the racist bus company
No time for her to pettifog
Against their Jim Crow sanctimony
Just because she was black
No reason to be ill-treated
Martha sat down on the only free seat
Reserved only for one who was white
Martha cared not a jot
She knew what was wrong
She sure as hell knew what was right
Martha planted her feet
Firmly on the ground

Then sat down on the seat
She was harangued by the driver
He told her to move
Because she was black
Martha was a sole survivor
She knew this was the time
It was not time to turn back
Her chance to take a stance
Grab this opportunity
To demand her share of dignity
Proving she was on the right track
Showing the world she was black
So when they called the police
Martha sat down to stand up
Against their racist caprice
She was no longer willing
To be treated like an animal
She was burned out
By the whipping and lynching
As if she was a criminal
Or worse as if she was an animal
Martha knew it was time
To honour her ancestors
And her descendants
For her to make a stand against
Being confined and ring fenced
By the cheap cloaked creepy KKK
Who killed her kinsfolk every day

And made her feel second-class
As if she was some kind of ass
She could not let it pass
It was time for a volte-face
Martha ignited her light
And struck some sparks
That years later spread
Throughout the land
Turning America on its head
She inspired MLK
She inspired Rosa Sparks
By lighting thedarkness
Martha held the torch that scorched
The racists in and out of court
Yes rest assured she was the one
Who had the guts to start the fight
To prove what is wrong
To show it cannot be right
To deny them treating her
As an animal and a criminal
As if it was a sin to be born with black skin
She was fighting for her kin
So the little lady from Baton Rouge
Who set out once and for all to prove
Her desert and dignity was no different
Than any racist just because of her birth

Though their prejudice was rife
Cutting her heart like a jack-knife
She refused to buckle or bend
She fought to the bitter end
She showed them she was right
She proved that being black
Was no different than being white
She would not be their whipped dog
Like them she had no reason to cower
She was more than some racist's cog
That was her potency and lasting power
That is the lifetime legacy of Martha White

Blank Heart of a Hunter

I remember the pure thrill of the kill
The sheer rush that shot through my veins
When I looked and saw your ruddy remains
I had to quickly turn away

Though I still feel the fun of that first kill
There's a difference I hate to confess
Today in some way I first saw death's mess
And knew you are no different to me

Al I recall is the hell of it all
When I looked deep into your eyes
And at once I counted how many lies
I still continue to tell myself

I was blooded by my dad as a cub
And I felt important that day
Yet what I know is the real rub
Since then I have lived a lie
In every way in what I do and say

Blue-bird sings the Blues

She flew through the unchained
Sky-blue countryside
Sparkling eyes and freedom's song
Spiralling and soaring wide
Twists and turns as nature's acrobat
On a wild glide wing
Her timeless tune is proof
The blue-bird was born to sing

A single shot from the one with a sawn-off soul
A single shot burst out to end her timed life's toll
A single shot in spring split her pain-filled sighs
Blasted the last blue-bird
From the blood-spilled skies

On her wing lies the bleeding shotgun bruise
In her eyes lies the stark dark spark of her muse
At once her shattered heart proves who to accuse
Denied her silvery voice leaves her no choice
Silently the dead-eyed blue-bird sings the Blues

Advocate

Noël Sweeney is a practising barrister who specialises in criminal law and human rights and animal law. He has lectured and written on all aspects of those subjects including in particular the legal role and status of animals.

While he has no real heroes in or out of the law, Sweeney has a defined admiration for Kurt Westergaard who drew the cartoon that was reprinted in the Charlie Hebdo magazine. Westergaard was neither cowed nor impressed by threats from intolerant people driven by religious zealotry. He wished to be remembered as 'the one who struck a blow for the freedom of expression.' His memory sits side-by-side with the activist stride of Martha White.